PATCHWORK
REALITY

PATCHWORK REALITY

HAPPILY MARRIED TO A SCHIZOPHRENIC

PAULINE HANSEN

PLAIN SIGHT PUBLISHING
AN IMPRINT OF CEDAR FORT, INC.
SPRINGVILLE, UT

ISBN 13: 978-1-4621-1364-4

Published by Plain Sight Publishing, an imprint of Cedar Fort, Inc.
2373 W. 700 S., Springville, UT 84663
Distributed by Cedar Fort, Inc., www.cedarfort.com

Library of Congress Cataloging-in-Publication Data on file.

Cover design by Angela D. Baxter
Cover design © 2014 by Lyle Mortimer
Edited and typeset by Whitney Lindsley

Printed in the United States of America

10 9 8 7 6 5 4 3 2 1

Printed on acid-free paper

TO CHANDY, STEVEN, LEVI, TYLER,
AND MARIAH—OTHERWISE KNOWN
TO EACH OTHER AS CHIMPY,
BROVINA, LIVLINT, GROLSH, AND JED.

I LOVE YOU LIKE CRAZY!

CONTENTS

ACKNOWLEDGMENTS

TO THE MANY EARTH ANGELS I HAVE BEEN PRIVILEGED to cross paths with:

To my favorite person in the world—I cherish and adore you, sweetheart! I sure am glad you went to that dance.

I am deeply grateful to my parents for more things than I can list, but for starters: to my dad, who taught me to work hard, appreciate nature, and love country life. To my mom, who taught me to live simply, be optimistic, and remember that there are no free lunches. I couldn't have asked for better parents than the two of you!

To my sister and best friend, Stephanie. Your unflagging encouragement is such a treasure to me, and so are you!

To Haley, Rod, Whitney, and the rest of the team at Cedar Fort. What a talented and amazing team you are! It has been an immense pleasure working with you.

To my writer friends and to those who read my manuscript and offered invaluable advice, especially Laura Bastien and Jennifer Holt. Thank you for your time, advice, encouragement, and kind praise.

And to my Father in Heaven, for his divine guidance, for sending angels to bear me up when I needed lifting, and for reaffirming to me in so many ways, time and time again, that I needed to write this book. I hope that means it will touch someone's life for good.

PROLOGUE

"Example has more followers than reason. We unconsciously imitate what pleases us, and approximate to the characters we most admire. In this way, a generous habit of thought and of action carries with it an incalculable influence." —Christian Nestell Bovee

EVERY DAY WHILE I WAS GROWING UP, I WATCHED AS my mom put everyone else's needs, especially my dad's, before her own. Mom would hold dinner until Dad came home, shush everyone if he fell asleep in his chair, and live with faded paint on the walls because the smell of a fresh coat bothered him. The five of us kids shared one bathroom, but we learned to wait if Dad was in there. Mom strictly forbade us to disturb him, even when we suspected he was only using the time to catch up on the *Reader's Digest.*

My mom's devotion ran deeper, though. She trusted my dad explicitly in religion, in parenting, and in every other area. She believed in him and his ability to lead our household. My dad, in turn, was totally devoted to my mother.

At one of my worst moments as a preteen, after my mom and I had argued about something or other, I yelled in frustration that I hated her. It was uncommon for me to do something like that, and, with concern, my dad came in my room to talk to me. The moment is seared indelibly in my memory. He didn't yell or even get mad.

He cried. And my dad seldom cried.

I never again, regardless of my frustration, told my mother that I hated her.

Once I matured, I wanted what my parents had, to fill my mother's same role as wife in the life of my future husband. It was part of a long-standing, unspoken tradition passed on from her own mother, as well as

1

from aunts and friends, and I considered myself privileged to be the next in line for the legacy.

Alan Watts said, "We seldom realize that our most private thoughts and emotions are not actually our own. For we think in terms of languages and images which we did not invent, but which were given to us by our society."

So it was with me. My desire to follow in my mother's submissive footsteps wasn't so much a conscious thought as it was the natural result of my upbringing. Once I married, I would honor and sustain my husband, just as my mother and grandmother had theirs, and, in return, I hoped to gain the respect and loyalty of my husband, just as I knew these existed between my own parents and grandparents.

It didn't occur to me then—and in fact for many years afterward—that my husband might be a fallible man. That he could be capable of the kinds of lapses in health or judgment that would make it difficult to trust him completely was an idea I had never entertained.

Which is probably why I was so blindsided when, twenty years down the road, I found myself in exactly that situation.

1

"Family is not an important thing. It's everything." —*Michael J. Fox*

I MET CURTIS HANSEN DURING THE SUMMER OF 1986. HE was as thin as a yardstick, stood just a few inches taller than me, and had brown hair and beautiful brown eyes, which directly contrasted with the blonde hair and blue or green eyes from my side of the family. His lopsided grin was adorable, even when years later he chipped a previously filled front tooth. His skin tanned easily, and he was as hairy as a monkey. My brothers had such fine light hair, so Curtis's dark brown arm and chest hair was new to me but struck me as very masculine.

We were married in February 1987 and made our home in St. George, Utah, the city in which my husband was raised and where I'd always dreamed of living. Visiting there as a youth, I came to love the lush greenery, the palm trees, and the blossoms that popped out in February, so much different than the snow and below-freezing temperatures where I grew up.

As weeks turned into months and then years, I found I couldn't ask for more in a husband. Curtis always put my needs above his own. His loyalty to me was a treasure. Not a day went by that he didn't tell me he loved me, and I him.

I felt like I was reciting the Scout motto whenever I told anyone about him. He's honest, dependable, trustworthy, sincere, and genuine. My own motto became, "To know Curtis is to love him," and it was true.

But just as with most marriages, things weren't always perfect at home. Really great, but not perfect.

They say opposites attract. Once we had lived together long enough to really know each other, Curtis found I was too trusting, and I discovered he was largely critical.

Far too easily, I gave everyone the benefit of the doubt, figured that people in general have good intentions, and trusted humanity to a fault.

Curtis, on the other hand, made it his business to single-handedly "fix" everyone around us, especially my siblings. He never said anything to their faces; he'd just talk night after night about their faults and short-comings and everything he felt they should do differently to improve themselves and their lives. He did the same thing with high-profile people and those in the media, always focusing on their flaws and imperfections. His views seemed radical at times, but at the same time mild compared with those being shouted back and forth on TV.

Rather than canceling each other out, these traits amplified and intensified each other as we fought to keep a balance in our marriage.

But I couldn't blame him for his obsession with finding fault. Curtis's father had been cold and impossible to please. Curtis spent many a night using me as a therapeutic sounding board as he described the impossible expectations his father had had of him and purged all the hurt that had built up. When I realized what he'd been through and the deep scars it had left, I was even more forgiving of his faults, seeing as he'd been seek-ing acceptance his whole life. I was more than happy to give it.

Difficulties and disagreements notwithstanding, our marriage seemed fairly normal for the first fourteen years. Nothing was out of the ordinary, even when I look back on it. We had a good thing going, and life, in almost every aspect, was better than good.

We had a child every two years, two girls and three boys. We worked hard to pay the bills. Curtis worked at the school district, with odd jobs on the side, while I worked the morning sort at UPS and delivered on Saturdays. I also took in a few children for day care and went to school part time. Life was busy, and with a large family it was also expensive.

As the kids grew, expenses multiplied. Raising a family, especially in an inflated economy like St. George, was difficult at best. As often as pos-sible, we created fun times with our kids that cost little or nothing at all, but even when money was tight, we made a point of enrolling the kids in soccer, piano lessons, junior wrestling, and other activities. With the chil-dren we took in for day care, we were able to bring in a few extra dollars for such things. Chandy, our oldest, took piano lessons from a neighbor, and she and the two oldest boys, Steven and Levi, played in the city soccer league. Tyler and Mariah, the two youngest, joined soccer too when they were old enough. Every Saturday in the spring, Curtis and I would go to their soccer games, then Curtis would practice moves with them in the backyard to improve their skills. It wasn't as competitive as some of the other leagues, but it gave them something to be involved in.

Summertime was blazing hot in St. George. One of our favorite things to do was stop by Arctic Circle for twenty-five-cent ice cream cones. Trips to the local reservoirs gave us another inexpensive way to cool off, but more often than not, Curtis took the kids to the school where he worked, and they'd play basketball or hula-hoop or badminton in the gym, which didn't cost a thing.

Wrestling dominated the fall months. For practice, but mostly just for fun, Curtis would lie on the trampoline and balance Steven and Levi on their stomachs up on his feet in the air, then they would wrestle and try to knock each other off.

Once wrestling was over in the fall, it was the perfect season to go fishing, one of Curtis's favorite pastimes. Frustration set in, however, when all the kids went; pebbles tossed into the water and all the laughter and chatter scared the fish away. Our oldest son, Steven, became the sole companion for future fishing trips, where his dad taught him the fine art of threading a worm on a hook and reeling in the fish.

Winter days in St. George were perfect for spending outdoors, with the temperatures rising at times into the sixties. While the trampoline was far too hot to jump on in the summer, it was perfect for playing on in the winter. Tyler, our youngest boy, and his two brothers had a favorite game they liked to play with their dad. They'd all be on the trampoline, with Curtis in the middle and the boys running in circles around the perimeter. Curtis would attempt to trip them with a pillow, which they would jump over or dodge if they could. They'd get completely worn out, mostly from all their laughing, but they'd still want to keep playing.

I loved how good Curtis was with the kids—not only our own but also those we babysat. He always made me feel pretty special too. He adored me and let me know it. He would call me every day from work, and the consistency of his phone calls became an integral part of my daytime routine. It was always good to hear his voice, and he would often share something funny he or one of his fellow custodians had done. I didn't know the other workers very well, but I recognized their names when we'd meet at the annual end-of-summer dinner and the Christmas social.

I adored my husband in return, and we both knew we were meant to be together. We liked to talk about how, during our first summer together, we'd had so many opportunities to meet, but it wasn't until the third time, which must have been charmed, that we came to know each other and began dating. We met at a dance, and my favorite thing Curtis says to me is, "I sure am glad you went to that dance."

Life in general was fairly uneventful until the fall of 2001, when a series of events was set in motion that would haunt and define our family through the fall of 2010. Nine years. It took nine years to ascertain what was *really* going on. And it all began with a dream.

2

"A man is a very small thing, and the night is very large and full of wonders." —Edward Plunkett

WE HAD MOVED SEVERAL TIMES SINCE OUR MARriage in 1987, our most recent move being from an area called Back Diagonal in St. George to the city of Washington, just east of St. George. In 2001 we were living on a small knoll they called Staheli Hill, surrounded by beautiful homes with manicured yards. Our reddish-brown brick single level with a garage and a ten-foot picture window in front was by far the nicest home we'd lived in. The backyard looked out across the street below and to the fields beyond. They were prime for development and regularly a hot topic at zone planning meetings. I hoped the housing development never passed—I loved the green fields.

Curtis worked from 11:00 a.m. to 7:00 p.m., so his mornings were often spent reading the newspaper, doing laundry, and watching Mariah and my niece, Livvy, while I worked the early shift at UPS. Curtis had a green recliner near the front door that he sat in to read, and that's where I found him when I walked in the house from work most mornings.

"How was work?" he asked as I bent to give him a kiss hello this particular morning.

"Fine, how are things going here?" I asked.

I was already headed into the kitchen when he reached out and took my hand, pulling me back to stand next to him. He gazed at me in complete wonder and amazement.

"What is it?" I asked. I could see he wanted to tell me something.

"I had the most incredible dream last night," he said in awe. The look in his eyes spoke volumes, and I found myself drawn to what he was saying.

"What was it like?" I asked.

7

"It was the most powerful experience I've ever had," he answered. "The prominent feeling I got from it was God's infinite love for his children," he added in a hushed voice. "It was incredible," he repeated.

"It sounds like it," I said, rubbing his back. I waited for a moment longer, but he didn't act like he was going to say anything else, so I left him to ponder while I went about my day.

Exactly one week later, Curtis caught me once more when I came in from work and exclaimed, "I had another dream." Again, his eyes lit up and his voice was full of wonder. "It was a lot like the first one."

"What was it about?" I asked.

"I'm not supposed to say, at least not yet. It feels too sacred to share. But I'll tell you what both dreams were meant to convey." He paused, and then, leaning toward me, he lowered his voice to a whisper and said, "Anything is possible."

As he leaned away from me, I glanced at his face, which held a look that seemed to say, "Do you realize the magnitude of this?" As he continued to express his feelings about what he had experienced, I could tell he had a firm belief that something special was happening, and it gave me goose bumps when he talked about it. He had no doubt that his dreams were significant, and although he wasn't sure why he was having such dreams, my trust in my husband's character and my belief in God gave me reason to believe there was substance to his experience. I couldn't imagine, though, why he would be having them. What did it mean? Where would it lead? It would be several months before I heard anything more about it.

***

"I dreamt that some of our neighbors have started a relief fund," Curtis told me a few months later. "They're taking in money on a charitable basis for a family in need. I really feel like we are that family."

"What? Seriously?" I asked in confusion.

"In my dream, there was a large yellow envelope that had over three hundred thousand dollars in it," he said in amazement.

"You really believe someone wants to give us three hundred thousand dollars?" I asked.

"*Over* three hundred thousand dollars," Curtis answered.

"But it was just a dream."

"This wasn't just an ordinary dream. I know it meant something," he insisted.

"Why us?" I questioned.

"Why not us?" was Curtis's answer. "Do you remember what I said I felt my first two dreams meant? Anything is possible! There's a group of people that want to bless us financially, I can feel it." He was trying hard to convince me.

Curtis had never given me any reason to doubt him previously. Our marriage had been built on trust and loyalty, and I had a deep and abiding faith in him. So as he insisted time and time again on the validity of what he was dreaming, I felt as though I should believe him.

Curtis's excitement grew over time as he began to think of the opportunities this fortune would bring. Far from the sports car or larger home that many would dream of, however, Curtis decided that he wanted to invest in food storage. "We need to be prepared for whatever the future might bring," he told me one day.

Just before Y2K, we had made a concerted effort to stock up on non-perishable food items. We were in charge of a community group effort at one time, gathering orders from our neighborhood and coordinating canning projects. Although we had canned endless amounts, it seemed, of wheat, beans, rice, and other goods, we had by now used much of what we had purchased then.

"We'll become proficient in food storage," Curtis declared with enthusiasm, "then we'll be able to share that knowledge with a lot of people." With this new line of thought, Curtis felt like he had stumbled onto his destiny.

"There are certain families I want to help," he explained, "who are good, honest, upright citizens but don't have the means to do more than just get by." The more people he came up with that he would like to help, the more reasonable it seemed that this money would be coming our way, since he was planning to put it to such good use. It was as if he had found his calling and was sure that the universe was on board.

"More and more people want to contribute," he said with conviction. "They're anxious to be involved." He told me this had been revealed to him in yet another dream.

"But why would people give us their hard-earned money?" I asked.

"Because they know we're going to do so much good with it," Curtis answered.

"How could anyone around here even know about our interest in food storage?" I asked. We had moved from the area where we'd done all the canning with our neighbors. None of our new neighbors would have known of our past experience. I explained this to Curtis.

"People talk," Curtis replied. "They know about us." He sounded so sure, but I wasn't so sure. We were only five or six miles from our previous neighborhood, but it was still hard to believe our reputation had preceded us, or that the donations would ever be so high.

"I still don't understand why anyone would give us their money," I pressed. I was doing my best to support my husband in this, but I found it quite difficult to believe that a large sum of money was headed our way. Short of winning the lottery or the sweepstakes, things like this didn't happen. Yet, Curtis kept insisting the information was being revealed to him.

"You have to realize how it is with those that are well off," Curtis explained patiently. "They often look for a charity to give money to so they won't get hit so hard at tax time." I'd heard of that before, although I didn't know if our neighbors would be considered in that category of wealth. We did live in a nice neighborhood, and the homes were somewhat upscale—ours being one of the smaller and more plain ones—but most of our neighbors would be considered middle class, not wealthy.

"How could you possibly know that they want to give money to us, though?" I continued my line of questioning.

"Because of the dreams I've had. They're too real not to mean something. Trust me," Curtis said. "We're going to receive a sizeable amount of money, and we're going to do a lot of good with it."

I still wasn't convinced, but that didn't stop Curtis. Before long, he began thinking about how to help entire towns become more self-sufficient and prepared. "Anything is possible" was his new motto. His excitement over this prospect was boundless. He talked about the possibilities all the time, and he often mentioned moving to the country to help the small, secluded communities get prepared for hard times. We'd always planned to move to the country someday, and now Curtis felt this was why we'd had that notion.

As strange as his new infatuation was, I was relieved that, with something new to keep him occupied, Curtis ceased to be so critical of everything and everyone. In fact, as time went by, he grew to appreciate and compliment my siblings rather than pick away at their faults.

But although Curtis was occupied with his dreams and how to interpret them, months went by and we hadn't received the money. So Curtis began predicting when he felt we would get the money. He told me that voicing his belief in it would increase the likelihood of it happening. He would give me a specific date, smile his knowing smile, and say "trust me." His first prediction was the end of the 2002 school year, before summer break.

Originally, he thought that only our neighbors were involved, but then he began noticing some strange things at work.

***

"There's a group of people that are pulling for us and want to support us financially," Curtis explained to me once during our daily afternoon phone call. He was a custodian at Snow Canyon High School, and he would call me on his break. "The people I work with might even be involved. But there's another group that has a different agenda, something I haven't quite figured out yet. I'm getting more attention than usual at the school, and at first I thought it was all positive, but it's not."

"What do you mean, more attention?"

"A lot of people I don't even know have talked to me lately, like a girl from yesterday. She's a sophomore, I think. I don't know if it's because I was nice to her or what, but today, she grabbed my hands, twirled me around, and said we were getting married!"

"Seriously?" I said. "How bizarre." I shifted the phone to my other ear as we continued our conversation. I had no idea how to assimilate the story. Curtis had never told me anything like that before, and him falling in with a high school girl was about the last thing I could imagine. I didn't know why she would say something so strange, other than to goof off, so I decided not to think much of it.

More often than not, though, our afternoon calls were totally ordinary. Curtis would share something funny that had happened at his work, often his doing, and often to his chagrin.

"How's my honey bunches?" he'd ask when he called.

"I'm good. How's my darlin'?"

Curtis groaned while laughing at the same time. "You need to lock me up and not let me out in public."

I laughed with him. "What do you mean? Why?"

"Ohhhhh, it was bad." He laughed again, good and hearty this time.

"What did you do this time?" He was notorious for making a fool of himself. I curled up on the couch to hear his story.

"So there's this teacher that was outside by the softball building where the coaches' offices are. I decided to try and strike up a conversation with her." He groaned. "Oh, man! I can't believe my stupidity. I'm serious. You need to lock me up, hon." He chuckled with self-reproach.

"Go on," I urged, imagining him in the custodial closet, kicked back in a chair with his feet up.

"She was unlocking one of the field offices, and I noticed that she had a big bunch of keys, so I told her she could probably get into more rooms than even I could, and that I was impressed with the authority she had. Then I really stuck my foot in my mouth."

"Uh-oh," I said, waiting for the punch line.

"'You could get in the coaches' offices,' I told her. 'You could steal their lunches!' The problem was, this lady weighs like three hundred pounds!" He laughed again. "You should have seen the look she gave me."

"I think I do need to lock you up and save you from yourself." I laughed along. "I'm kidding. I love you like crazy anyway, blunders and all."

Those were times when things seemed natural and fun. There were always days, weeks, sometimes months in between Curtis's more serious moments when he would talk a lot about his dreams and what he thought they meant. When he brought up his dreams, I would tell him I felt he was giving them too much meaning, but he would always try to convince me otherwise.

The predictions became a source of awkwardness too. Summer came and went without his first prediction coming true. School was about to start again, so Curtis decided that would be the next best date to predict. The kids needed things for school that we didn't have the money for right then, but Curtis would hint that soon we would be able to get them anything they needed. He even promised the two oldest kids he would pay them a hundred dollars for every A they earned on their report card that year. After hearing this, Chandy, our oldest child, had some questions.

"You've never given us that much for our grades in the past," Chandy said, "so how could you now?"

"Trust me," came her dad's reply.

"But where will you get the money?" Chandy asked. "You and mom have always hinted that we have to be careful with money. What's changed?"

"Don't worry about it, Chandy. Just get good grades at school. That's all you need to be concerned about."

"I hope I can get at least two As," Steven spoke up. "That way, I'd have enough money to buy a Game Boy Advance!" He obviously wasn't as concerned about where the money would come from.

In private, when we had retired to our bedroom that night, I spoke my mind. "How could you make those promises when you aren't certain how things will turn out? We don't have that kind of money, and you know it." We'd paid the kids one dollar for every A on their report card in the past—but never a hundred!

"Trust me," was his reply once again. "We need to voice our belief and then show faith that it will happen." I had never had reason before to doubt my husband's sincerity, and he was certainly sincere about his dreams and what he felt they meant. Still, until it panned out, I felt that getting the kids' hopes up was unfair.

Sure enough, when report cards came out, we had to dash their hopes and admit we couldn't pay up.

***

Curtis kept predicting dates for when we could expect the money, but when one would come and go without a yellow envelope, he'd tell me he was just off on the timing, then he'd set his heart on a different day. I insisted, though, that he be more discreet this time rather than involving the children. I hated seeing them disappointed.

His latest prediction was that something would happen by Christmas 2002. I tried to ask him to let things happen as they happened, but he felt that the predictions were necessary, like telling someone you want to lose weight so they hold you to it. I was skeptical.

Imagine my surprise, then, when one day we came home from church and saw something on our doorstep. I had a hunch what it might be.

"Tyler, Mariah," I said to my two youngest children, "I think you might want to go check what's on the front porch." Steven and Levi perked right up and ran as fast as they could toward the front door. "Hold up there, boys," I said, as I came down the walkway. "Take it easy," I warned, since they'd already started clawing through the box of goodies someone had left for us.

Chandy was fifteen years old by then, her maturity showing in her ability to patiently wait while the other kids sifted through the goods.

"Look, there's a stocking for each of you with your name on it," I said. The rest of the items were ingredients to make a complete Christmas dinner: ham, potatoes, stuffing, carrots, and other items. Curtis was excited that something, anything, had happened, but it didn't take long for him to feel like there was much more to come. The way I saw it, a Secret Santa gift was a far cry from $300,000, and it felt wrong to even try to compare them. In other words, I felt we should be grateful for what we did receive, rather than comparing it to what Curtis thought we would receive.

As much as Curtis wanted to believe the Secret Santa gift was from an unnamed group of charity givers and that it was just the tip of the iceberg, so to speak, I had inadvertently discovered the giver by regifting a candle in the box to Curtis's aunt. I learned a good lesson then: it is unwise to regift items of unknown origin.

I let Curtis know about my discovery, but he passed it off by saying, "Maybe my aunt is involved with the group." I didn't know how that could have been possible, but as with everything else lately, anything was possible.

Just like always, Christmas was my favorite time of year. We made treats for the neighbors and hung the stockings from the mantle. In keeping with tradition, we opened one present on Christmas Eve, usually pajamas, and then woke up at 6:00 a.m. on Christmas morning to open the rest of the gifts. I remember leaving the tree up clear through January some years, since we rarely used the living room and it wasn't in the way. I also remember getting a surprise gift that year from my husband: a ring to wear on my wedding ring finger, since the diamonds had fallen out of my original ring and we didn't have the money to get it fixed. I knew that my new ring had cost fifty dollars since I had shown Curtis a similar one I wanted for twenty-five dollars and had seen the one he chose in the display, but he had splurged and bought the higher-priced one. I cried when I pulled it out of my stocking, and I still wear it on my ring finger.

***

Spring came early, on the heels of a typical mild St. George winter, and then summer hit with a vengeance. By the end of May it was 109 degrees and a horrible time for our cooling unit to go out. We bought a window air conditioner and put it in the kitchen window, then hung sheets in the doorways to keep all the cool air in the family room, where we all slept for a couple of nights while we waited for our new air-conditioning unit to be installed. A very welcome gift, a check for one thousand dollars, came in the mail from Curtis's brother, who lived in Colorado. Once his brother had heard about the failure of our cooling unit, he pitched in to help us purchase a new one. Curtis didn't try to tie this gift in with his predictions, though. He knew how big-hearted his brother was and gave credit where credit was due.

Summer came and went and Curtis's most recent prediction, the beginning of the new school year, went by too. I would ask Curtis not to make any more predictions because all it did was make us both anxious; me because I still couldn't wrap my head around his vision, and him because he felt so strongly that something was going to happen that he felt like he was letting me down when it didn't. I tried to tell him that I wouldn't feel let down if nothing ever happened. We had a good life, and I was happy with the way things were. He too was happy with our life, but his desire to help people kept him believing and hoping that we'd get the money that would make that possible. He insisted that voicing his predictions showed he had faith and believed, and when you believe, you receive.

Curtis soon found another radical way to show he had faith. I had been saving money in a wooden jewelry box I kept in the bedroom and was excited to see it had grown to a fairly sizable amount.

"Look," I said to Curtis one night just before bed. "I've saved seventeen hundred dollars so far. We've never saved that much in our lives."

I don't remember Curtis's reply; I just remember what he did. In the coming weeks, he began taking money from the box and spending it. If he felt we needed more groceries in the house, he'd go buy some. He stocked up on rabbit feed (we kept a few rabbits in the backyard) and purchased a few more rabbits. He used some of the money for repairs on our vehicle, which I would have otherwise budgeted into our regular monthly expenses.

When I finally discovered what he'd been doing, I was livid! "What's the meaning of this?" I demanded.

"It's a way to show faith that we have money coming our way," Curtis explained.

"You have got to be kidding me!" I yelled.

"Trust me, hon. I know what I'm doing."

He was in the doghouse for a few nights, to say the least.

***

The heat held on forever but finally started cooling down around Curtis's birthday in October 2003. This would be his fortieth, and for the first time ever, I had planned a surprise escape for the two of us: rafting down the Colorado River, a Canyonlands-by-night river trip, and two nights in a motel in Moab, Utah. Curtis and I had never gone on a trip meant for just the two of us—not even a honeymoon. This would be a first.

I had the reservations all set and was just waiting for the confirmation in the mail. Ninety-nine percent of the time, I was the one to check the mail, so when Curtis got it the one day I didn't want him to, the day the confirmation came in the mail, I couldn't believe my misfortune. At first, I thought the surprise would just be ruined, but we'd still have a great time. Things didn't work out that way, however.

Curtis's brother called to let us know that he was coming out from Colorado for a visit at the same time we were going to be on vacation. Curtis always put me first, so I figured that we would go on our trip as planned, but suddenly his conviction that something wonderful was going to happen for us was inexplicably connected, in his mind, to his brother's visit, as though his brother would have something to do with it after all. He insisted we needed to stay home that weekend, and I was forced to cancel all of the reservations I had set up. *Nothing out of the ordinary is going to happen, and we're canceling our vacation for no reason,* I thought, but I knew it was pointless to argue. Curtis had made up his mind.

The weekend with his brother sailed by without a single hint of something spectacular happening like Curtis thought it would. I tried to tell myself I should be glad we saved the money we would have spent on the trip, but that wasn't consolation enough to soothe my disappointment. I began to resent Curtis's dreams and predictions. Before then, with the exception of the children's disappointment about not getting big bucks for their grades and the money he had spent from our savings, his dreams hadn't really interrupted our lives. I hadn't been invested and didn't believe enough to be upset when his predictions proved false, but having to cancel our trip began to push me over that edge.

***

Life, for the most part, continued normally. Our children were growing, now ranging from age seven to sixteen, and two small bedrooms wouldn't accommodate the five of them much longer, so we decided to sell and look for something bigger. The unpredictability of the St. George economy gave us no idea when we could expect to sell, so we decided that once we had secured a buyer, we'd begin our search for a new place.

After our home had been on the market for about six months, a middle-aged couple made an offer. We had to find a new situation, and quickly, but there wasn't anything in our price range to buy, and rentals were scarce. We didn't have a choice, though; we had to move out, and all that was available and affordable to rent were apartments and an old, ugly fourteen-by-sixty trailer. Apartment living was out. We'd lived in an apartment before and hated it—cigarette smoke drafting up through the vents, neighbors through the wall having shouting matches at all hours of the night, music so loud it made our lampshades shake. So we rented the trailer with a plan to look right away for another home to buy. Only a six-month lease was required on the trailer rental application. We could survive anything for six months. Couldn't we?

3

"A house divided against itself cannot stand." —Abraham Lincoln

THE LIGHTNING STRUCK. EACH TIME THE THUNDER cracked, the windows would shudder and rattle. The screech of the wind whining through cracks was like a dying bird.

It rained buckets—outside *and* in.

"I need another pot!"

"The pots are all taken."

"Then bring me a bucket or something—whatever you can find!"

The rent was cheap. That's all the ugly old trailer had going for it. Unusual though it was, the trailer had a basement that had been dug out from beneath it, with a black iron spiral staircase leading from the main floor. My seven-year-old spoke her fears.:"It feels like there's kidnappers in the basement." She was right; it did.

Living in "The Box," as I dubbed it, felt like living in a black hole. Not only did we live in the most horrible place we'd ever lived, but Curtis was gone a lot, either at work or staying after to help coach the track team. I wasn't working, and when Curtis and the kids were gone and I was alone, my nerves took a beating. The trailer had a bad feeling to it, and I was relieved when Curtis and the kids came in each day.

One evening as we were preparing for bed, Curtis broached an old undesirable subject.

"It's happening again," he said.

"What is?" I asked.

"The people I work with and even some of the students are acting kind of funny, like they have a secret."

"Do you think it's good or bad?" I wondered, though I was only asking to be nice.

"It will be a blessing in our lives," he answered confidently. "I can feel it. By Christmas, New Year's at the latest, something good will happen."

Resentment lingered from having to cancel our mini vacation a couple of months previous, and, knowing how disappointed I was, Curtis hadn't said anything to me about his predictions since then, which was a welcome relief. This newest prediction only grated on my nerves. I huffed a sigh, fluffed my pillow, and turned my back to my husband.

"Good night, sweetie," he said dejectedly.

"Good night," I said in the same tone.

"I love you," he whispered.

"I love you too," I managed.

My thoughts skimmed over what he had just told me. Curtis had previously predicted the gift we'd receive would be from a group of strangers, but now it looked like he was focusing on the students and faculty at the high school where he worked. None of it made sense to me, but it seemed so clear to him.

Who specifically did he think was planning something? Curtis had worked at Snow Canyon High School for over four years, and I knew, from all the stories he had shared from work, that he was well liked. He would tease the football players and the cheerleaders, have whole classrooms of kids sing "Happy Birthday" to the teacher (even though it wasn't even close to their birthday), and help kids when they couldn't open their lockers. He loved to sit with the disabled kids for lunch. He'd even tease the blind kid about a cute girl that was ogling him or tell him that his lunch had spilled on his shirt. Curtis liked trying to pull the shy kids out of their shells. He'd get Christmas cards and graduation invites from the kids he'd made an impact on. He had a good rapport with his coworkers too, but I couldn't imagine that any of them would want to do something special for us.

It soon became apparent, however, just how *many* friends Curtis had at the school when, about a week before Christmas, I got a knock on the door in the middle of the day. I was still in my housedress with no makeup on and my hair in a mess.

On my doorstep were about four teenagers, who I found out later were members of the student body council from the high school. They all yelled, "Merry Christmas," then proceeded to hand me bag after bag of groceries: a ham, potatoes, boxes of stuffing and cans of gravy, cans of green beans and boxed desserts, and a bag of oranges and another of apples. I was so overwhelmed, I don't even know if I thanked them properly. Later, as I was going through all the items, I found a cup with cash totaling $838 and Walmart cards for everyone in the family with $100 on each card. Everything was marked "Secret Santa."

What a miracle it was! I was so grateful for the Secret Santa gift that I sent a large thank-you card to the school to put in the office in the hopes that those involved would read it and know of our gratitude.

It was an uncomfortable feeling, though, to be on the receiving end of a gift like that, especially when I thought of the way I was dressed at the time the students came to the door, combined with the horrible dump of a box we lived in. It made me feel like a charity case.

Like trailer trash.

And living in The Box was getting worse. Now that Curtis had some further positive reinforcement with his predictions, he began to spend a lot of time trying to figure things out. He would sit on the couch with a journal and a notebook for hours each day, scratching down thoughts and names. Soon, his interaction with me and the children was next to nothing. Since it was winter and it was forever raining, we were all cooped up in the house together, yet I still felt lonely. Steven spent his time downstairs on his computer. Chandy and Levi were almost always out with friends. Tyler and Mariah were still young, and, frankly, I can't remember what they did with their days. Evenings were always better than the long days when everyone was gone. Still, I began missing my husband's companionship. I had to wonder what it was Curtis wrote down for hours on end, and, feeling ignored and pushed aside, I decided to bring it up. "What's all that writing you're doing?" I asked him.

"I'm recording my dreams so I won't forget the experiences I've had," Curtis answered.

"It sure does take a lot of your time. Isn't there something else you could be doing?" Frustration tinged my voice, and my body language spoke volumes as I placed my hands on my hips.

Curtis stiffened and shot me a look of defiance. "This is what I need to be doing right now," he said as he jabbed a finger into his notebook.

"The kids could use some interaction," I tried again. He didn't back down.

"There are three things that are important to me right now: my dreams, my journal, and my family," he stated succinctly, ticking them off on his fingers. He went back to his writing, effectively ending our argument.

Being last on his list did something to my psyche. I didn't like feeling important by default. It wasn't just the words, though; it was his actions. Curtis spent hours each day writing in his journal and notebooks—it was more than a ritual; it was an obsession. He even told me that he asked in his prayers at night for more dreams—they made him feel inspired, directed. The family? We were just the default.

I know we decorated for the Christmas season, although the cheery decor did little to perk up the old place, but I don't recall Christmas Day—what we gave the children, waking up, unwrapping presents.

Those were dark, forgettable days. Gloom hung over us like dirty clouds. I was still unemployed, having spent the last year as a stay-at-home mom, and living in The Box became torture. Days and weeks crawled by in oppressive monotony, with the interaction between Curtis and me deteriorating rapidly. After another month of staring at the bleak, black paneling confining me, I was desperate to get out.

I'd heard that good money could be made cleaning homes. I was ready to try anything. When I mentioned the idea to my neighbors, they said they had a coworker who could use a cleaning lady.

Hank was a lonely, bipolar, divorced man in his fifties. He needed a cleaning lady—and a friend. I needed validation. So began our acquaintance.

I started cleaning his condo on Wednesdays, with phone calls in between. The calls were originally intended for scheduling purposes but eventually extended to a broad range of subjects. Stimulating adult conversation lit a tiny glow in my otherwise dreary world. For the most part, Curtis didn't pay any attention while I talked to Hank on the phone, but after a couple of lengthy phone calls, Curtis had some questions of his own.

"Who was that?" he asked.

"It was just one of my new cleaning clients," I answered.

"You seem to have a lot to talk about."

"Yeah, I guess so. He asked me about a recipe he was trying. He wanted to know if I'd made anything similar and that led to other things. No biggie." I shrugged my shoulders.

Curtis seemed slightly bothered, and I didn't want to upset him any further, so I let Hank know that calling my house number was off limits after that. We began to communicate through notes left on the entertainment center at his place.

***

It was 2004 and spring came early like always in St. George, and a picnic sounded like the perfect outing to jump-start the season. I explained to Curtis how isolated Hank was and that he would most likely appreciate an invite, and since I hadn't given him any reason recently to resent Hank, he readily agreed. Claiming Dutch oven pork chops were his specialty, Hank even did the cooking.

I was in my second semester of Japanese at Dixie State College, where I was working toward my associate of arts degree. Hank had lived in Japan as a young adult, so I asked him to help me with my homework and my final project, a speech I had to give in front of the class spoken only in Japanese. After cleaning his condo, I'd wait for him to return from work so he could help me with my Japanese.

With all the help he'd given me, I felt I owed him something in return. He often expressed how solitary his life was and how much I meant to him, so one day I thanked him with a hug. This became our parting ritual after that. I began stopping in here and there to say hi, and soon, we were fast friends. He was easy to talk to and lavished me with praise.

We had Hank over for dinner one night. He got up on the roof with Curtis to adjust the float on the swamp cooler while I finished preparing the meal. The evening didn't go over very well, though. Some of Hank's philosophical views made Curtis uncomfortable—something about using your mind as a tool to control your life. The concept was a confusing one, but I sat there smiling and nodding my head, since it *sounded* smart. Once Hank left that evening, though, I discovered Curtis had gotten the wrong idea. He thought my smiling and nodding was a display of how enamored I was with Hank, and no matter what I said, I couldn't convince him otherwise, and in the end, Curtis said it would be best if I didn't clean for Hank anymore.

We needed the money, though, and, if I had to be honest, I didn't know if I could give up the attention. Curtis was still off in his own world of journaling and dreaming, so despite having a husband and a family, I often felt lonely. I also felt bad for Hank and was afraid that severing my friendship with him would break his heart. I pled my case to Curtis, but it bothered him that I was standing up for Hank and still wanted to work for him. That changed, though, when Curtis had a dream just before I had to go clean for Hank again.

He dreamed that if I were to end my friendship with Hank, there was a chance Hank might take it so hard that he'd end his own life. Not wanting that kind of guilt hanging over our heads, Curtis relented and gave me permission to keep cleaning for Hank. That, in turn, translated in my mind as permission to visit him outside of work. I hadn't built my cleaning clientele much yet, so I still spent more time in The Box than I would have liked and used any excuse I could think of to get out of the place. I called Hank one day with a schedule change, and then I told him I had a treat for him and would drop by later that evening.

"Come on over anytime," Hank replied. "I'm addicted."

"What do you mean?" I asked, although I was pretty sure I knew what he meant.

"I'm addicted to you, and now I can't get enough."

What woman doesn't want to be told they're an addiction? I too was hooked—the compliments, the stimulating conversation, the attention. It was one time I was actually glad for Curtis's dreams. If only I knew what I was getting myself into. My desperation for companionship blinded me to the signs.

**

After six long years of juggling family, work, and college, in May 2004, I finally graduated with my associate's degree. It was just a two-year degree, but I was thrilled! The summer of 2004 flew by. The rain dried up during the hottest months, and since we didn't have any plans for a family vacation that summer, we opted instead to get a pool pass at the aquatic center, which would give the kids a way to cool off and have some fun. Curtis never wanted to go, so I'd drop the kids off at the pool, but, rather than going back to The Box and suffer in the deafening silence, I would visit Hank. I occasionally mentioned to Curtis that I would be stopping by Hank's house, with the excuse that I was dropping something off or whatnot, but more often than not, I used the "don't ask, don't tell" way out. I knew deep down that it wasn't appropriate for me to be spending so much time alone with an unmarried man, but by then my loneliness had thrown my good sense all out of whack.

During our time together, Hank and I would cook up something Japanese or watch a movie or listen to music. Or just talk. Back at The Box, Curtis and I rarely talked. Anytime I tried to express my need for some companionship or my thought that he spent far too much time thinking and journaling in solitude, he'd curtly remind me that what he was doing was important. He continued to scratch away in his journal, but lately he wasn't as prone to share his thoughts with me. There were, however, occasions when he found it extremely necessary to communicate with me, like the time he told me about a dreadful, frightening experience that he'd had.

4

"It seems we are capable of immense love and loyalty, and as capable of deceit and atrocity. It's probably this shocking ambivalence that makes us unique." —John Scott

WAS LYING IN BED LAST NIGHT," CURTIS TOLD ME, "AND suddenly I felt like there was a huge, crushing weight on my chest. I couldn't breathe, and the pain was horrible. I could feel an evil presence, and it had something to do with Hank. The only way I was able to stop the crushing feeling was to sing a church song over and over again."

"Really?" I said with sympathy. "That sounds awful." After all the unusual things he'd shared with me in the past three years, I knew he felt that the message was supernatural or divine in nature. There was no denying his sincerity and the gravity of his expression.

"I don't want you to clean for Hank anymore," he stated. "I have a bad feeling about it."

I was in full alarm mode. My reluctance to give up the friendship I'd built with Hank overrode my interest in my husband's premonitions. I began to defend Hank. "It can't be all that serious. I don't feel like I'm in any danger."

"I know what I felt, and I know it meant something. Believe me when I tell you that it's not a good idea to go there anymore." His tone of voice brooked no argument, but I wasn't ready to give up.

"I can't just up and quit. What would I give as the reason?"

"Tell him anything. I don't care. Just don't go back!" Curtis was beginning to sound desperate to get through to me. He was raising his voice, which was rare for him. I still didn't back down.

"We need the money," I argued (even though I had built a pretty decent clientele by then), "and Hank could really use a friend." I still felt bad for Hank in his friendless world, and to turn my back on him felt like breaking a commitment.

Curtis wasn't the type to threaten divorce after every little spat or argument, but this was one time that he went over the edge. He felt very strongly that I shouldn't go back to Hank's, so when I disregarded his advice, he started packing a suitcase. I'd never been so scared in my life.

The tears were falling down his cheeks as he put socks and clothes into the suitcase. "It's either him or me," Curtis challenged.

"Why does it have to be that way?" I argued.

"It just is. You have to make the decision."

"Of course I don't want you to leave!" I cried.

"Then you have to promise you won't ever go there again."

"Okay, okay." I gave in. "I won't."

I had my sister take over the job of cleaning Hank's condo so that at least he still had someone cleaning for him. I loved my husband dearly, so even though I'd felt neglected as of late, I knew it was only a bump in our marriage. Things would work out sooner or later.

Although I wasn't talking to or seeing Hank anymore, he still remembered my birthday, which was a few weeks after I had stopped cleaning for him. He brought back the bag of rice and the dark blue blanket that I had let him borrow and sat them on our front steps with *two pounds* of milk chocolate mint truffles, my favorite.

I broke down and called Hank to thank him for the chocolates. He said he missed me and begged for a visit. I gave in and began secretly seeing Hank. It felt horrible living a lie, but Hank's pleas for friendship got the best of me. I hated the deception and felt uncomfortable, but things hadn't gotten any better at home. Curtis was still unavailable as a companion. I had hoped he would come to the realization on his own how much he was neglecting me, but when I brought it up and it didn't help, I felt like I was on my own.

Hank, on the other hand, was unusually perceptive. He was able to *feel* when I was having a bad day. He knew things about me that I don't know how he could have known. At first, this seemed like an unusual and bonding connection we had. I didn't foresee it might become dangerous.

***

Fall turned into winter, and the rain started up again. So did the leaks. Our landlords lived hours away and were rarely in the area, and the roof repairs they did attempt hadn't helped any. The Box should have been dubbed The Sieve—we'd often have pots under half a dozen or more leaks.

It was like Chinese water torture. *Drip, drip, drip.*

My need to get out of The Box was consuming. I told Curtis I was going for a walk, but I didn't want to be alone, so once I was out the door, I called Hank on my cell phone and told him to meet me around the block.

Rounding the corner by the baseball fields, I walked up to his car, opened the door and slid in. We went for a drive in the rain.

Christmas was coming, and Hank would spend it alone. My sympathies went into overdrive, and when Hank asked for just one thing for Christmas, a kiss under the mistletoe, I didn't see the harm. It would be just like in the movies, right? I wouldn't say it was just like in the movies, though—we were more like two statues with their lips together.

After that, Hank started wanting more than I was comfortable giving; talking on our cell phones at least once a day, holding hands when we were together, more kissing. I was uncomfortable with the level of affection he desired. Up until then, we were just friends spending time together. Now that things were changing, I reminded him I was a married woman. He insisted the affection he desired was just a way to express a high regard for each other. No harm implied. That's not how I felt about it.

I wished I had stayed away, but I was in deeper now. Hank had seen that I was willing to put him before my loyalty and honesty to Curtis and knew I was seeing him on the sly. I think that must have given him some ammunition.

I could tell Hank always anticipated when I was thinking of pulling away from him; he knew exactly what my weaknesses were, and he would use those against me whenever I would reduce the frequency of my visits and phone calls or act uncomfortable with his excessive affections. He'd play on my sympathies or give me gifts he knew were my favorites.

Hank once told me that each person who comes into our lives either plays the part of a savior or an adversary.

Things had changed, and Hank had ceased to be a boon or blessing in my life. I knew it was time to get out of the predicament I was in, but that was easier said than done. Especially after a conversation Hank and I had one day.

"Is your husband okay?" Hank asked me.

"What do you mean, is he okay?" I asked.

"Is he well? Does he have any conditions that may possibly be life threatening?"

"No, he's healthy as a horse," I answered.

"Hmm, that's strange," Hank mused.

"What's strange?"

"Here's another question for you," Hank said. "Does May twenty-first mean anything to you?"

I thought for a moment but couldn't come up with anything. Hank just shrugged and let it go with that.

As I thought about the conversation, my imagination got the best of me—was he alluding to my husband's demise?

Suddenly, I knew I was in way over my head, but had no idea how to get out. I was already uncomfortable with the romantic turn my relationship with Hank had taken, but now it felt *dangerous*.

Then something happened that put everything into perspective. Chandy needed to borrow my cell phone and while she was using it, a text arrived from Hank. Chandy felt his words of flattery were inappropriate and sent him a return text saying that he was a freak, that I was a married woman, and that he shouldn't be texting me.

The next time I saw Hank, he told me what Chandy had said, and suddenly, it all became clear to me. I could either have my family, or I could try to "save" Hank. I couldn't have both.

Someone else would have to save him because my family meant more than anything to me, and even though my husband was still treating me like a default, I'd be okay with that for now. I said good-bye to Hank and never went back.

Within a couple of months, my secret relationship with Hank all came out in the open, and, under intense questioning, I told Curtis everything. When I saw the hurt in my husband's eyes and realized how my deception had affected him, my guilt was acute. With tears running down my cheeks, I apologized again and again, ashamed that although I had felt so lonely, I would hurt the one person I cared for the very most in the world.

Curtis softened and realized he had played a big part in my need to seek attention elsewhere. He apologized many times for getting too involved in his own world and finally understood just how shut out I must have felt. In the end, we were both able to learn from the experience and realize that we needed to work together as a team and be number one in each other's lives.

We began making a concerted effort to plan a weekly date night and do more things together. We went on long walks and talked a lot. We rebuilt our trust in each other, and Curtis began to open up once again about what he felt were blessings headed our way. I didn't necessarily want to have to listen to all his predictions again, but it was better than being ignored and pushed aside.

***

Knowing The Box was only a temporary housing arrangement, we were still trying to find a home to buy and settle into, so that became our new focus. We'd always loved the small town of Veyo seventeen miles north of St. George. It was about ten degrees cooler there but was still close enough to town for shopping.

We found some land with owner financing and then, after telling our real estate agent we planned on putting in a new manufactured home, she talked us into calling a builder she knew that would build us a custom home for cheap. The plans were drawn up, and all we needed was the go-ahead from the mortgage company. We came within a week of closing the deal, but suddenly our builder called and told us he had just received calls from at least five of his subcontractors, who told him the cost of materials had just gone up.

He wouldn't be able to build us our home for the price he had originally quoted.

We hadn't sealed the deal yet, so we took the new figures into the mortgage company and came away with bad news. We didn't qualify for the higher amount.

My disappointment was acute. I lived the following few weeks just going through the motions. I had wanted so badly to move out of The Box.

Besides cleaning residential homes, I had taken a job with Jensen's Property Management, but I hated cleaning dirty apartments. I was scrubbing the floor of one of those apartments one day, thinking about our predicament. Curtis's job paid decently well, but it didn't stand much of a chance against the inflating economy of 2004–2005 in St. George. There were no nice homes for a lower price; we'd end up back in a dump if we were to try to move.

I felt trapped, like we were beating our heads against a wall trying to make ends meet. Everything felt so hopeless that I couldn't help but cry as I worked. I was depressed, tired, and hungry, and I admit that at the back of my mind, I almost wanted to seek comfort at Hank's condo. As muddled as I was, I still knew that was out of the question, so I returned to the house listlessly, hating the thought of spending any time at all in The Box.

Curtis must have had a sixth sense that I was having a horrible day because without even calling me first, he came home in the middle of his shift to see how I was doing, which was something he had never done before. We went out on the trampoline to talk. I couldn't bear to stay in The Box.

"Don't worry," he soothed, "I have a feeling it won't be long now until we'll get the money we've been waiting for. We'll be able to move anywhere you want."

Here I had hoped Curtis would soothe my aching disappointment, but instead he triggered my pent up hostility. "You can't seriously be counting on that, can you?" I said in disbelief.

"I *am* counting on it, and so should you," Curtis said.

My disappointment in not getting our new home and land in Veyo was just too much. "It's too uncertain. I don't want to talk about it anymore!" I lashed out, getting up and stomping into the house.

Once inside, I looked around and knew right then and there we had to find somewhere else to live. We'd already stayed twice as long as our original lease of six months, so in December 2004, almost exactly a year to the day from when we had moved to The Box, we found a home to rent in a very nice housing community called Ironwood. The rent was considerably more, but we were ready to live in a home again, a sanctuary.

Our new rental used to be the model home for Ironwood, the interior designed for high traffic and low maintenance. I didn't like the industrial-ish looped Berber carpeting, but the tiled kitchen and bathroom counters and floors were beautiful. It felt good to live in a nice home again, one I enjoyed coming home to after a long day's work.

***

A couple of months later, in February 2005, we were at Applebee's celebrating our eighteenth anniversary. Once we had ordered our meals, Curtis struck up a conversation. "Living in that old trailer sure took a toll on our family," he said.

"Ain't that the truth," I replied.

"It cost us some momentum in The Game," he continued.

"The Game?"

"I've discovered that what we've been experiencing since that first dream I had is all set up like a game, and we're the players. I haven't figured out all the details, but I'm learning more and more all the time," Curtis said.

And here we go again, I thought. It had been nice for the past two months not to discuss his dreams. But they were always lurking in the shadows.

"While we lived in The Box," Curtis said, "I was trying to force things to happen, but I didn't feel as inspired. I wanted the dreams to continue, so if they slowed down, I felt I needed to do something. At one point, I felt like I should be more expressive, talkative, and show more gratitude to everyone I associated with, because I feel there are people combining efforts for us, and I need to show appreciation for their efforts." He shook his head then and said, "There's still a group of people wanting to take us down, though, and you-know-who is behind it." That's what he called Hank, among other more colorful things.

"You think so?" I asked. Ever since the strange conversation with Hank when he had inquired about Curtis's health, I had a nagging worry, so I wondered in what context Curtis thought Hank was involved.

"I dreamed that Hank and Chandy's boyfriend wired our new house just before we moved in, so watch what you say while you're at home," Curtis cautioned. Chandy had a boyfriend who was an electrician's apprentice. Curtis glanced up as the waitress approached our table with our meals and switched the subject to something else.

My mind was still on what he had claimed, though. I didn't seriously think our home had been wired. I mean, doesn't that only happen in books and movies? I gave his notion the slightest bit of credit because there *are* people who have had their homes wired, but then I immediately disregarded it. No way were we *that* interesting. This became just another one of those things Curtis was a bit radical about, and it was easy to brush it off.

Curtis said he had dreamed it, though, and he continued to trust his dreams, so although I didn't believe it, as an outward showing of support on my part, we began only talking about The Game when we went out on dates or went for walks.

Later that spring, Curtis began feeling that there was yet *another* intrusion in our lives.

Curtis was an assistant track coach at the high school. Several boys were on the team, but for some reason, he ended up coaching mostly girls.

"It's the strangest thing," he said, when we went for a walk one evening. "Out of the moms of the girls I coach, I swear there's an unusual amount of single ones."

"What does that have to do with anything?" I asked him.

"You're gonna think I'm crazy," he said.

"Shoot."

"I feel, especially lately, like there is more and more of an effort to separate us. It's been like this from the beginning, but even more so now. How could it be a coincidence that there are so many single moms of the girls I coach?"

"If someone is attempting to separate us, then there has to be more going on than just being a single mom. Are they doing anything to try to seduce you?" I asked with a bit of sarcasm.

"Yes!" he said. "They show up in their tight little shorts and tank tops to watch us practice, and they've got half their chest hanging out. I know they're doing it on purpose."

"Scandalous!" I exclaimed with a smirk. My husband is indeed very handsome, but I figured it was common knowledge he was married. They'd just make fools of themselves if they tried making a play for him.

Our walk had brought us to a bare construction lot that was being leveled for a new housing project, and in the growing dusk, Curtis scratched a figure in the dirt with a stick: $4,000,000. He quickly erased it.

"What in the world?"

"The Game is growing," Curtis said as he glanced over at me, his tone suddenly serious. "There are more players now, and that's how big the pot has grown. I've discovered that it's turned into a test for us. Single men and single women are wagering to see if they can get us to separate. That explains all the single women that have suddenly shown up around me and why you went through what you did with Doofus." I felt a sick smoldering in my stomach any time I thought about or was reminded of the dark events we lived through during our time in The Box. How had I ever found myself in such a compromising situation? Yet Curtis had just said that he felt it was a part of The Game. Like maybe it was orchestrated. That didn't seem possible.

"But why us?" I asked. "Why would we be singled out for a test like that?" We started walking again, slower this time. Curtis occasionally swung the stick at a small rock to send it sailing away from us.

"Because we're people of importance," Curtis explained. "That's why the pot has grown so large. There's a lot of interest in the results of The Game, and we're going to have to be fiercely loyal to each other to win."

I was skeptical, to say the least, and not just a little perturbed by the whole mess. People of importance? Four million dollars?

5

*"Desperation is the raw material of drastic change. Only those who
can leave behind everything they have ever believed in can hope to escape."*
—*William S. Burroughs*

I DECIDED NOT TO LET GRANDIOSE THOUGHTS OF SUD-
denly receiving millions of dollars tilt my perspective. I was determined
more than ever to live in the moment. Life was good. We were happy
and healthy. What more could we want?

Curtis wasn't ready to give up on his dreams, though.

"How's my favorite person in the world?" I said as Curtis came in the
door from work. It was late in the year 2005.

"I'm good. How's my honey?" Curtis asked, pecking me on the cheek.

"Great." I smiled. It had been a good day, one of the rare few I had off
now that I had built my cleaning business to nearly full time.

"Do you feel like going for a walk?" Curtis asked. This had become
code for "I want to talk about The Game, but not in the house." I silently
groaned. I didn't want him to ruin the good day I was having.

"Sure," I answered anyway, trying to keep the discouraged tone out of
my voice. "Just let me get some shoes on." I grabbed my jacket on the way out.

The kids were all old enough to be on their own, except maybe
Mariah, but one of her older siblings was almost always at home, so Curtis
and I had freedom to come and go as we pleased.

Once we were on our way, Curtis started talking like I thought he
would. "Did you know you're a woman of destiny?" he asked with a sincere smile.

"What do you mean?"

Instead of answering my question, he asked me something else:
"Do you think we can handle being people of influence?"

"I guess I haven't thought about it before," I answered.

"I really feel like we need to give it some consideration. Right now, before things happen. I don't want money to change us."

"Don't you think we should wait until something happens?" I asked. "Like they say, don't count your chickens before they hatch." So many predictions had fallen through since Curtis had his first dream, and I was sick of talking about it. "I think it's time we put The Game to rest and just let things happen naturally," I continued. "If something's gonna happen, it's gonna happen, with or without us hashing it out or making predictions about the timing."

"That's not how I feel about it," Curtis countered. "I feel that talking about it shows we have faith in what we believe is going to happen."

"It hasn't worked so far," I pointed out.

"You have to admit I've been right about quite a few things," Curtis reminded me. "Like the time we got Secret Santa on Staheli Hill, and again just last year when we got Secret Santa from the kids at the school."

"Okay, I admit you've been right some of the time, but I still think we should let things ride for awhile. I'm tired of talking about The Game. In fact, maybe we could just forget about it." We had just rounded the corner by the baseball fields, which reminded me of something else I'd like to forget.

My husband shook his head adamantly. "We can't just ignore The Game. It will never go away. We have to see it to the end."

Never go away.

See it to the end.

These phrases began to echo in the recesses of my mind. I felt trapped again. As far as I could tell, there *wasn't* an end. It would *never* end.

Desperation drove me to devise an otherwise unthinkable plan. I was in fight-or-flight mode.

In essence, I tried to run from The Game.

I thought that if we moved far enough away from the orchestrators and the other players involved, we could leave it behind us. A good day's drive would be nice. A different state, even better. At first, I didn't tell Curtis this was why I wanted to move. Instead, I used the inflated economy we lived in as an excuse and talked him into starting over somewhere else. Surprisingly, he agreed to the move, and on a wing and a prayer, we packed everything we owned in a fifteen-foot moving truck and headed for Idaho.

It was late in February 2006. Once we reached our destination, we stayed in a motel the first two nights and found a rental home by the third night. Curtis got us settled into our new rental and then took the Greyhound back to St. George, where he would finish out the school year at his job before joining us in Idaho.

The city was surrounded by countryside—potato farms, to be exact. We went driving once to look at a home that was for sale, and all we could see for miles and miles were potato farms. There were small rolling hills but no mountains, and my sense of direction was thrown completely out of whack. Wherever I'd lived, I had always been surrounded by mountains, and I had used them to know which way was north. It was very disconcerting to not have them as a guide. I needed my mountains.

My sister and her kids made a trip to visit us within the first two weeks we lived there. On her way, she picked up Curtis and brought him for a visit, even though he'd just helped us move recently. Unaccustomed to the snow as we were, ours was the only snowman on the block, and the only full-blown, all-out snowball fight commencing in the backyard.

Just before they left, my sister shared some disturbing news with me. "Curtis and I were talking on the way up here, and he told me that he secretly asked the kids to pray for a way to move back to St. George."

"What!" I cried. "He didn't!" My sister nodded. "Then why did he agree to move here in the first place?" I asked, fuming.

She shrugged. "He made me promise not to tell, but that's hardly something I could keep from you," Steph said.

I was livid, but I didn't want to reveal that Steph had said anything, so I tried a roundabout approach when I spoke to Curtis about it.

"Are you gonna give it a chance up here?" I asked him.

"We're here, aren't we?"

"But are you committed?" I pressed.

"We have to see what I can find for work first. I don't know how things will turn out."

I could tell he was avoiding commitment, but I left it at that. I knew I wasn't being completely honest either because I hadn't told him the real reason I had wanted to move.

Only three weeks had gone by when I broke my leg ice skating. I still remember lying there on the ice, looking up at my three children who were standing over me, looking scared. Mariah covered her face with her gloved hands and cried, "No, Mom!"

The home we had rented was set on a small hill and had a huge set of cement steps leading to the front door, and navigating the steps, the ice, and the snow with my crutches turned out to be nearly impossible. I ended up using the sit-and-scoot method.

I rarely went out, though. For five long weeks, I lay in my white bedroom, staring at the white ceiling, watching the white snow fall outside. The silence was deafening. I thought I'd go mad.

I couldn't stand to lie in my bedroom any longer; I wanted to be out in the living room where I could mingle with my family. We found a furniture store and bought a red recliner.

Someone's prayers to eventually get us back to southern Utah must have been answered, because circumstances found us moving in with my parents in Cannonville, my tiny hometown in southern Utah, for my recovery. Our moving van was chock-full when we moved to Idaho, so to add the new recliner we had purchased meant leaving something else behind. We had a large computer desk that we decided we could do without, and we left it in the rental home.

Curtis had kept his job at the school the whole time I was in Idaho with the kids. Now that our plans had changed, it was nice to know that he hadn't made any ripples in his occupation. We agreed Idaho wasn't meant for us, but if Curtis thought that meant he could dive right back in and talk about The Game and make more predictions, he had another thought coming. I already felt I'd been prayed a broken leg. I certainly wasn't going to fall right back into the same routine of worrying that the house was wired or being told we were going to receive four million dollars. My loyalty and devotion toward Curtis had been a bit shaken with his pray-to-move-back stunt, and I now felt less inclined or obligated to trust his every word and action.

"You will *not* speak of The Game—not now, not ever," I insisted the next time he brought it up. He could tell I was serious. After that, for *four and a half years*, he didn't speak a word, and I began to hope we'd left it behind us. I soon found I was living with a false sense of security, however, and that he had only suppressed talking about the things that were still raging in his head. But while the false security lasted, I enjoyed my reprieve from The Game.

***

Once I'd recuperated at my parents' home, we needed to find a place to live. Curtis's work was on the far west side of the St. George area, so we moved to the smaller outlying town of Ivins, located on the west, just past the St. George city boundaries.

What a sweet blessing it was to live in Ivins! The red mountain that stood as sentinel on the north was such a welcome sight every day. I couldn't work at first, so I took the summer off and finished writing a novel I had been working on. Once my leg had healed sufficiently, I began cleaning again for the women I had cleaned for previously, and I also worked four days a week at a bookstore.

In July 2007, after living in one side of a duplex for a year, we found what we felt was a perfect fit for our family: a tri-level with five bedrooms located on the south end of Ivins in a neighborhood with large family homes in cul-de-sacs. We were finally in a big home, and I didn't plan to move anytime soon. In fact, I had what I called my ten-year plan. Mariah still had eight years of school and two of college, so I wanted to stay in our new home for at least that long. I hoped I would never feel the need to flee again.

Our new home was what I'd always dreamed of. It had a wide front porch with white spindle railing and shutters on the grid windows. The kitchen and living room were open and roomy, and although the back-yard was small, it still boasted plum and apricot trees, grapevines, and plenty of room for the trampoline.

That September I turned forty. I worried it would be difficult, but I was too spoiled to even think about my age.

Chandy invited me to visit her place, an apartment on the campus of Utah Valley University in Orem, Utah. We saw the movie *Hairspray*, went shopping at Ross, and came home to a surprise birthday party she had planned for me. The next morning, I found that she had written, "Honk, it's my birthday!" on my van windows. It took me a minute to get used to so many people honking at me.

We'd lived in our new home for about five months, working to get certified for foster parenting—something we'd wanted to do for quite some time—when we found out that Curtis's mother needed a change of living condition. Having suffered from fibromyalgia for decades, she'd done fairly well through the years with the help of her husband, but his recent confinement to a care center had changed things, and she was going downhill fast. Where she had previously been an excellent conversationalist, she now rarely spoke. She had red rings around her eyes, and the skin on her face had begun to sag and droop, most likely from all the medication she took. We decided to take her into our home to try to help. As much as I knew I wasn't going to like it, she was only fifty-nine years old. It seemed like we had to at least try. She had so much life left to live, if we could just help her lose some weight and reduce her need for so much medication.

Curtis had recently taken up a great interest in vitamins and herbal supplements. He had a thick book called *Prescription for Nutritional Healing* that gave many types of ailments and listed herbs, vitamins, and minerals that could be taken for each ailment, plus other home remedies to ease pain and suffering. With a new patient to work with, Curtis began an even more in-depth study of each and every ailment that his mother was taking medication for: hypothyroidism, anxiety, high blood pressure, schizophrenia, water retention, fibromyalgia, insomnia, pain, heart trouble, and others I can't even remember.

I wasn't used to having another adult living with us. It felt intrusive and uncomfortable with Curtis's mother in our home. She rarely spoke; she just stared as I walked by. I began prolonging my workday on purpose. Christmas was especially awkward because she slept on the sofa in the living room, and that's where we wanted to gather for opening presents. I was glad when the day was over.

In January 2008, we got our first call placing foster children in our home. Two beautiful blonde-haired, blue-eyed girls came to live with us, ages two and four. The girls kept me busy while I tried to ignore the growing anxiety I felt having my mother-in-law in the house.

I think my daughters must have known I needed a break from her because to our pleasant surprise, when Curtis and I came home one day after shopping together, Chandy, Mariah, and Mariah's friend Caroline had made us a candlelight dinner. Everything was set up in the living room, with a sheet hung between it and the kitchen for privacy. Curtis's mom sat in her wheelchair in the kitchen, where the girls had insisted she stay, but as soon as we walked in the door and she heard Curtis's voice, she started calling for him, begging for some meds. Miraculously, he ignored her.

As the girls brought in our first course, we found that they had even dressed the part. They each wore black slacks, a white dress shirt, and a green tie. It was all so unexpected, and Curtis even had tears in his eyes. That started up my waterworks, but we were able to tease each other and laugh it off and enjoy our delicious meal together.

Curtis knew I didn't like having his mother there, so he would attempt to cheer me up by leaving me love notes. He'd done this a lot through the years, more often than I had, admittedly, and one of my favorites was when he turned over a yellow note pad and wrote on the cardboard backing, "You're beautiful, inside and out." Underneath, Steven had written, "Aww, thanks, Dad. Steven."

I laughed out loud and tucked it away in my special box.

Curtis loved to make me laugh! He once wrote a note and stuck it to a bag of rolls in the fridge. It said, "You have nice buns." Funny thing was, my mom came to visit right then. She saw it before I did and chuckled.

Three months went by, and Curtis's mother was still living with us, but one day in February that changed. Curtis pushed his mother outside in her wheelchair so that she could enjoy some sunshine and fresh air. She had lost quite a bit of weight by then and was looking much better. She was talking again, and she spoke words that were music to my ears.

"I feel like it's time to move back to The Meadows. I miss my friends," she said.

I admit it was a huge relief she wanted to leave. I'm sure she struggled living with us just as much as we did having her there.

Once she left, I didn't want the couch in the living room anymore. It had come with her when she moved in, but she wouldn't be able to fit it in the smaller apartment she was moving into, so she'd left it behind. I ordered it into the garage and replaced it with a couch from downstairs. Her recliner from downstairs found its way into the van and off to the thrift store.

Curtis kept in close contact with his mother after she moved out; they would talk on the phone at least twice a day. She'd tell him what she suffered from the most, whether it was pain, sleep deprivation, anxiety, or something else, then he would study and read about each thing so he knew how to help her. If he read about a new herb that he thought she could benefit from, he would purchase it at the health food store, which he kept her debit card for. He would take the new items to her, often going to her house clear across town two or three times a week. She did help pay for gas, but I started resenting the amount of time he spent taking care of her. As months went by and nothing changed, I began to feel pushed aside again, like when we lived in The Box.

"I need your help at home," I complained one day while I was drying apricots. Alone. Again. "You're gone a lot, you know."

"I have to help her. She's my mother. I owe her a lot. She's the only one that kept me sane while growing up," Curtis argued back.

"There's a certain point, though, where it's too much. Can't you find a better balance?" I pled. We had four foster children by then, and with our own five children, that made eleven of us in the family. Shopping, cooking, cleaning—it was all a major production, not to mention picking and preserving fruit when it came on.

"You did the same thing with Doofus. You felt like he needed a friend, and your overly compassionate nature went into overdrive and you had to try to rescue him," Curtis said.

"That was then. Right here, right now, I've been home, right where I'm supposed to be, taking care of what I'm supposed to take care of," I returned. "You've always said that your family is the most important thing to you. Prove it!"

"My mom *is* my family," he practically shouted.

"And she's taking up *far* too much of your time and energy! I'm telling you, I need more help at home! Your mother will always need way more help than anyone can possibly give her."

"I have to do what I can for her," Curtis insisted.

"Then why don't you go move in with her? You can be two little peas in a pod and drown yourselves in the study of herbs!" I grabbed my bucket and stalked out the back door, slamming it behind me. When the apricots were on, they didn't wait for hypochondriac mothers or doting sons.

6

"I think a dysfunctional family is any family with more than one person in it." —Mary Karr

E HAD MOVED A LOT IN A FEW SHORT YEARS— from Staheli Hill to The Box to Ironwood, then our short jaunt to Idaho, then to my mom and dad's, then to a duplex in Ivins, and now to our new tri-level. Because of that, we had neglected reading scriptures together as a family like we had done in the past, so now that we felt settled for a change, we began to read again in the mornings before school.

There wasn't quite enough seating in the living room for everyone, but Curtis would sit in the red recliner (he adopted it as his own once I didn't need it anymore), I would sit on the piano bench, and the kids would all squeeze onto the couch. When Chandy was gone, it wasn't too bad to squish four kids on it.

We had the same four foster children in our care for nearly a year—a brother-sister sibling set and two sisters from another family—so it became necessary to have the younger kids sit on the floor for scriptures.

***

It had been over a year since his mother had lived with us, but Curtis was still spending a lot of time trying to figure out what would help her the most. I complained often enough about how excessive I felt his attention was that he finally took all the bottles of herbs to her house and tried to teach her what to take, when, and how much. He still did a lot of directing over the phone and went to her place once a week or so. It must not have been enough attention for her because then she started a hospital antic.

It was the third time in a couple of weeks that she called us to come and get her at the hospital and give her a ride home, and it looked awfully fishy, like she was just doing it to get attention. We were already taking her at least once a week to see her husband at the care center, about five miles from where she lived, *and* we took her shopping every other week. Now she was pulling this hospital stunt, saying she had heart palpitations. Even though Curtis's brother and his wife were sharing the responsibility of her care, we still got plenty of calls from her.

"Every time your mother says jump, you jump." I was complaining again.

"She's in the hospital!" Curtis was losing his patience. But so was I.

"Still, you know she's doing this on purpose. You can't just jump at her every whim. It's never ending, and it's getting worse. Can't you see it for what it is? She just wants attention and isn't getting enough, so she's making up new reasons to call you for help."

He continued to insist on helping her, but finally, the calls started slowing down. His mom was doing a lot better than when she had lived with us. She had lost over a hundred pounds and could now walk with a cane. She began to go shopping with the group from her assisted living home every Thursday, and from what I heard from my older children, she was lively and talkative again. I was glad to hear that, but I was still unable to bring myself to visit her. I wasn't bitter or hateful toward my mother-in-law; I was just at my limit. It was tough having her live with us. In addition to the arrangement feeling intrusive and awkward, she'd spit out her food after tasting it, saying it was nasty, and there were nights she'd wake us up for more sleep aid.

It turned out that Curtis's loyalty had its limits too.

"I can't believe you spent over three thousand dollars on herbs, and they didn't even help," his mom said one day when she was talking to him on the phone. Curtis felt like he'd been slapped.

He had been working with his mother for nearly two years by that time, which was early in the fall of 2009, and the results were astounding. I'd even seen her shopping on her own at Walmart, where I hid behind the apple bin in the produce section and secretly watched her. She didn't need a cane to walk anymore, and yet his mother had the audacity to say he hadn't even helped her?

Curtis tended toward extremes. After processing the phone call and letting it sink in for a few days, Curtis did a complete one-eighty. His solution? Stop talking to his mother altogether. He felt like if he were to ever talk to her, even just casually, he would be sucked into her never-ending health problems again.

Not too much later did Curtis finally realize that all the hours he'd spent trying to "save" his mother from her ailments—all the time he'd spent away from home when he'd gone to her place—had been detrimental to our marriage and family. He apologized profusely and told me that he would never let that happen again. He had always considered himself fiercely loyal to me and to our children, and to have the shocking realization that he had let something get in the way of that made him take a closer look at his priorities, especially after what we'd been through when we lived in The Box.

I wasn't going to argue. If Curtis didn't want to speak to his mother, that was fine by me. She must have known how stubborn Curtis was when he made up his mind because she didn't bother us anymore.

This, however, eventually led to Curtis not speaking to any of his family. He said he had his reasons, but they weren't totally clear. It was true that he had never had a good relationship with his father, so that wasn't anything new.

"I was only eight or nine years old," Curtis told me one day, "and I worked at the service station my dad owned. There was a contest for the cleanest Union 76 in the country, and the family who won would go on a trip. I was raking the weeds in the back. The hillside sloped down and was black because that's where they used to pour the old oil when they changed someone's oil. Every twenty to thirty minutes, I would go inside to the drinking fountain, and after doing that a few times, my dad asked, 'What ya doin'?' in an agitated voice.

"One of his coworkers, who was a state wrestling champ, defended me and said, 'The boy is just thirsty. It's 111 degrees out there!' The other workers could go inside when there wasn't anyone at the pumps and sit under the air-conditioning.

'He doesn't need to come in that often,' was my dad's reply, and he told me to go on outside and get back to work." Curtis said after that, he wouldn't admit hot or cold, or even pain. He would ignore his body telling him when to stop.

I guess Curtis figured he'd done his best where his family was concerned, and now it was the season to let things be. It was good to have Curtis's help around the house. Finally, we felt like a complete family again, and our focus was on our children for a change.

Chandy was off to college, Steven was graduated and lived with us, Mariah would be a teenager in a few months, Tyler was a freshman, and Levi, our middle child, was a junior. Plus we still had three foster children in the home.

Levi had been the child that was "stuck in the middle" all his life. He wasn't the oldest or the youngest, the oldest boy or the youngest boy. He was the only one with blue eyes; all the other kids had brown eyes like their dad. At sixteen, he was finally the tallest, but that only lasted until Tyler passed him up. Levi had picked up a rebellious streak from the effects of the middle-child syndrome, and if there were any spats among the siblings, you could be certain Levi was involved. I had always had a soft spot for Levi, though. He had been such a mild toddler compared to Chandy and Steven, and he knew just how to melt my heart—like the time we were all out on the front lawn eating popcorn and counting the stars as they slowly came out in the twilight. He wrapped his arms around me from behind and said, "Thanks for the pizza, Mom." I had made homemade pizza for dinner, and his sweet remark made it worth the effort.

Levi always managed to do little things like that through the years, but as he got older and became a bit of a nuisance, Curtis could only see that side of him.

Curtis had taken it upon himself to knock the "nonsense" out of Levi whenever he acted up. If he picked on his siblings or hogged the computer, Curtis would punish him in some way. In my mind I could picture a scale of fairness, and, as far as I was concerned, it was far from balanced. Levi had more chores, more punishments for not doing his chores, and fewer privileges compared to our other children; hence, I became Levi's advocate.

Once a pendulum begins to swing, it seems to pick up a momentum of its own. The more I defended Levi, the harder Curtis was on him.

By his junior year, Levi was old enough to get himself up each morning for school, but if something went wrong with his alarm or he forgot to set it, I felt that it was our job as parents to get him up. One morning, I asked someone to go see if Levi was awake yet. Curtis was completely against anyone waking up Levi. He insisted Levi needed to be responsible for getting himself up at the right time.

Needless to say, Levi was late for school.

Levi didn't rebel against his father's authority until his late teenage years, and then he would only try to defend himself, not outright disobey or ignore his father. One day, though, Levi was asked to do the dishes (whether it was his turn or not, I don't remember), but he was found lounging in his room long after he had been assigned the chore. Curtis barged into Levi's room and began a yelling match with him. Levi got so upset that he punched a hole in the wall.

At some point after that, we were all getting ready for school and work one morning. Three of the four foster children were at the table eating while I tried to keep the baby out of the cupboards. Mariah had already left because her school started earliest. Tyler was in the shower. Levi was nowhere to be seen. I wasn't about to suggest someone go get him up, though.

Curtis noticed his absence and asked where he was. I said he was still in bed.

"Why hasn't someone woken him up?" Curtis asked.

"You said he needs to take responsibility to get himself up," I said incredulously.

"But if he doesn't wake up on time, someone has to go get him up," Curtis replied indignantly.

"You've got to be kidding me!" I practically yelled. Was it my imagination when he had gotten so upset the time I tried to intervene?

"He can't be late for school!" Now Curtis was raising *his* voice.

I was so mad I picked up the plastic mixing bowls that Zyon, one of the foster children, was playing with and, one by one, threw them as hard as I could across the kitchen while I screamed. The foster kids were wide-eyed with shock, but I kept it up until I ran out of bowls. It was very rare that I lost it like that, but the way Curtis was acting had driven me absolutely up the wall.

The foster children were gone by September, so we were back to just the six or seven of us. Chandy lived at home off and on, depending on whatever else she was doing. We made sure to have family pictures taken during one of the times she was home. It was late November 2009 and nearly too cold to have pictures taken outdoors, but they turned out great. I ordered an eight by ten of each of the kids and one of the family and then arranged them on the west wall in our living room. Looking back at our smiles, it's obvious that we were totally clueless as to what lay ahead.

7

"But for me, it was a code I myself had invented!
Yet I could not read it." —Erno Rubik

I T WAS MAY 2010. THE PHONE RANG, AND THE CALLER ID
said "Schools Public," so I thought it must be Curtis calling.

"Hi, is this Pauline?"

"Yes."

"This is Mary from the high school."

"Oh, hi, Mary." She worked as a secretary in the office.

"I was just calling to see if everything was okay with Curtis."

"Didn't he show up for work?" I asked in surprise.

"Yes, he's here. That's not the problem," Mary answered.

"Oh, good," I said.

"It's just that he hasn't spoken to anyone for about three weeks now."

"Really?" I replied. "How odd."

"I know," Mary said. "Do you know what's going on with him?"

A thought occurred to me then. "Curtis did mention at the last custodial meeting that they were told to be careful about talking to the students, especially the young women because of their tendency to make
more of it than they should, then faking that they are being sexually
harassed."

"Well, yes, it's true they did say that. I just didn't think anyone would
take it to such extremes," Mary exclaimed.

"I guess Curtis is just being careful," I replied.

The school year was over a couple of weeks later, so I soon forgot
about that conversation. Summer vacation arrived again, a nice break
from the school-day routine of getting the kids up and out the door. The
summer schedule also offered a reprieve from the same old grind for the

custodians. The everyday vacuuming and sweeping of the school year was replaced by cleaning vents and filters and waxing the floors.

About midsummer, we decided to take a break from everything: work, the heat, the daily grind. We headed north for Yellowstone and Glacier National Park.

It turned out our two-week road trip was the best vacation we'd ever had. No stress, no worries. Curtis can get pretty impatient with things like six-dollar hot dogs at Disneyland or kids that all want to stop at a different fast-food place to eat, but this trip, he was miraculously patient and agreeable.

Maybe those two weeks of pure bliss are what got me through the next four months of hell.

Curtis returned to work once we got back from vacation, and it seemed like a fairly normal summer until he started going to the school on Saturdays. At first, it was just for an hour or so. He said he was going in to work out, which was a normal occurrence; for years now, he'd gone to the gym at the school to work out. It was when he was gone for two, three, sometimes four hours or more that I began to wonder what he could possibly be doing all that time.

I admit there was a nagging worry at the back of my mind that Curtis was seeing someone else. I would dismiss the thought almost before it could fully form, however, because that was something I could not imagine Curtis doing. But then I would think, "Yeah, but he's still human." I never thought *I'd* find myself in a compromising situation, yet I had been sucked into it, little by little. Even though I didn't have an affair, it was far too close for comfort.

Rather than stew about it, I knew I had to bring it up. I didn't want to be too overt, so I tried the roundabout approach.

"Hi, darlin'," I greeted him as he came home one Saturday afternoon. "How was your workout?"

"It went pretty well," Curtis replied innocently.

"Boy, that was a long workout," I exclaimed.

"I didn't work out the whole time," was his reply.

"You didn't?"

"No."

Hmmm. This wasn't getting me anywhere.

"So, what did you do the rest of the time?" I asked.

"I had some things I needed to catch up on."

He left the room to go into the kitchen and find something to eat, effectively ending the conversation. I didn't push it, but when he was gone even longer the following Saturday, we had a similar conversation, ending again with him saying that he had some other things he had needed to do. I pressed a little more.

"What kinds of things?" I asked.

"Figuring things out," he said.

"Figuring what out?" I asked, confusion lacing my voice.

"Things I need to be aware of that are going on around me."

"So, how is it that you figure them out while you're at the school?" I asked, still perplexed.

"Code talk," he replied.

"Code talk? What kind of code talk?"

"You've heard about the guys from World War II who had to speak code talk so the enemy couldn't understand them? It's kind of like that," he answered.

"Who are you talking to?" I asked.

"Those who are working for good."

"Like who?" He was being so vague that I couldn't grasp what he could possibly mean.

"People who are trying to find out who has ulterior motives. Influential people who support us as a couple," he answered.

At this point, I was so confused, I wasn't sure what to ask next, but a nagging feeling told me it could be connected to The Game. I had hoped we'd left that behind. It had been such a long time since Curtis had said anything about it. During the following week, I thought about what he'd told me so far, and by Saturday I had more questions, especially since this time he was gone for five hours.

"You were gone a long time," I said casually after he'd eaten and settled into his red recliner. I tried to keep the accusation out of my voice, knowing that if I wanted any answers, I'd have to tread carefully.

"Yeah, time got away from me," he answered.

"Did you get some more things figured out?" I hoped that if I acted like I understood our last conversation, he might expound some more.

"Yes and no," was his reply. He sounded frustrated. My curiosity was now full blown.

I still didn't understand the whos or hows of it all, but I decided to start with the whats.

"What kinds of things did you figure out?" I asked.

"Oh, things like the color of shirts certain kids wear to school, or the way they turn their bodies when they're standing in a certain place."

"Why would you try to figure out those kinds of things?" I asked.

"They all mean something," Curtis explained.

"And you say you're talking to who again?"

"Part of a group that's trying to do good. A charter, basically, that's hard to trace so consequences can't come back on them. It's a loose-knit yet organized group, and it's very large."

"So, how do you talk to these people?" I asked.

"Like I said, code talk," he replied.

"Can you tell me more about it, or is it top secret?"

"I can't tell you anything unless you ask me the right questions."

This sounded like something from the movies. *Or the mafia.*

"Is it illegal?" I asked in horror.

"No, it's not illegal," he answered, a little too seriously.

"So, do you use a computer to communicate with them?" I couldn't picture him pecking away at a computer keyboard because he was about as computer illiterate as you can get, but I didn't know what else it could be.

"No."

"Do you use walkie-talkies or something?" I continued.

"No, nothing like that."

We were at a standstill again. He wasn't volunteering more information, so I waited until the following weekend to ask more questions. I didn't want to bring it up, didn't want to talk about The Game, but with the amount of time he was gone, I couldn't ignore it.

"It's a machine in a closet at the school," Curtis finally told me when I pried him about how he communicated with this group.

"A machine? What kind of a machine?" I asked.

"There's pipes going up the corners of the room, and when I ask questions, there are electrical surges, on the right for yes and left for no."

My husband talks to a machine? For the sake of getting more answers, though, I played along. "How did you figure out what would be yes and no? How do you know it wouldn't be left for yes and right for no?"

"Because I asked something that I already knew the answer to."

That made sense, in a weird kind of way. "But how can someone be on the other side of a machine, answering your questions?"

"They are. Believe me, I know what I'm talking about. I've tested it, and when I just sit there and don't say anything, the machine is completely silent, but as soon as I start asking questions, it starts up."

I couldn't fathom how that could be possible, but he was talking and that was a good thing, so I continued my line of questioning. "So what kinds of questions do you ask?"

"A little bit of everything," Curtis answered. "I can't ask the same question twice or I won't be able to keep asking questions."

"How do you know that?"

"I *asked*," he articulated. His voice carried a tinge of something in his voice—annoyance, frustration? My time was up again. At least now I knew where Curtis had been spending so much of his time, although I didn't know what to think about him sitting in a closet for hours on end asking questions to some unknown group that he could only talk to through a machine.

Not having spoken of The Game for many years, and with life sailing along as normally as it ever had, this most recent occurrence seemed very strange. But with nothing to compare it to and having no experience with such things, I again attempted to explain it away with the thought that I knew Curtis was somewhat radical and had his own way of thinking. I had built a lot of trust in him through the years, so when he would insist he knew what he was talking about—would even *promise* me that he did—I didn't necessarily believe him, but I was willing to let him continue his own thinking process. It was sort of like agreeing to disagree. He knew I didn't believe what he was saying, but that didn't deter him.

Like when I mentioned that he was spending a lot of time away from the family on his day off, insinuating that he had more important things to do than sitting in that closet, he got upset and said that he was doing it all for the *good* of our family. This was unsettling but irremediable. Curtis was stubborn.

My distress was multiplied in the following days. I had assumed that his work week was still regular and uninterrupted, but by the end of the week, Curtis would come home frustrated and in a bad mood. Curtis was rarely in a foul mood, so I thought I'd see what was up.

"How's work going?" I asked him. The kids were usually out with friends in the evenings during the summer, so we had the living room to ourselves.

"Lousy," he admitted.

"What's going on?"

"People are trying to make things harder for me at the school. Things have changed; it used to be that the group I was talking to was all good, but now they're practically all bad."

"You mean, the people you talk to in the closet?" I didn't want to bring it up, but I felt like I should show some sympathy for what my husband was going through.

"Yeah. I got so frustrated, I stood up and kicked over my chair. I thought I had a lot of things figured out, but I'm starting to get mixed signals."

"I thought you only went in the closet on the weekends." Curtis hadn't been coming home any later than usual, so if he had been spending time in the closet, it would have had to have been on the clock.

"I've been spending one to two hours a day in there during my shift."

"What?" I said in shock. Curtis had never been dishonest about his work day before. This was highly unusual. "Does your boss know about this?" I asked.

"Yes, he knows, and he *wants* me to be there." He explained it as though he was doing a great service by figuring out the things that he learned while talking to the machine.

"Are you sure?" I asked, perplexed.

"I promise, I know what I'm doing," he said condescendingly.

That didn't seem right, but Curtis had just promised me he knew what he was doing, so once again, I left him to his own way of thinking.

I briefly wondered whether I should go to the school and ask someone about the situation. If Curtis found out I'd done that, however, he would be absolutely livid, and I'd never hear the end of it. Besides, how do you go up to your husband's boss and ask, "Did you know Curtis is sitting in a closet speaking to a machine? He claims you know he is and that you *want* him to." This was beyond the strange or radical things Curtis had done through the years, things that I had gotten used to by degrees. This was too strange to talk about, so I kept it to myself.

Things weren't always strange and tense, though. Curtis still called me every morning from work. He went to work early, so he'd call me before I'd leave to go clean houses. There was one morning phone call that we will joke about forever. I didn't answer when he called, so he left a message on the answering machine that said, "I hope you're on a walk and not still in bed." He knew I went walking quite often in the morning. I totally took his message the wrong way, though, so when he returned home from work that day, he asked me if I got the message he left.

"Yeah, what was that? A fat joke? 'I hope you're on a walk,'" I mimicked in a snarky voice. "You'd better not still be in bed like a lazy butt."

The total and genuine shock that registered on his face immediately let me know he hadn't meant it like I thought he had.

"What? No, that's not what I meant!" Curtis frantically explained when he realized how I'd taken it. "I just hoped I wasn't waking you up with the phone ringing. Aw, man, I'm an idiot."

"Oh!" I laughed, relieved. "I should have known what you meant. You're always considerate like that." I shook my head. "Sorry about that," I said with another laugh.

It was good to laugh.

But the Saturday just before school began, he spent *seven* hours at the school. I was frustrated and uncertain, and whether I wanted to be or not, it looked like we were entrenched in The Game again. Curtis didn't try to talk to me about it this time, though. Apparently, he still took it seriously when I had silenced him about The Game several years prior. The only time he said anything was when I asked him questions.

Curtis still spent a lot of time at home scratching name after name in notebooks. When we lived in The Box, he wrote more journal-type entries and only wrote names in the margins, but as time went on, he began to write full pages of just people's names. Sometimes it was initials, other times he would describe someone, such as "tall blonde girl." Names were often repeated, especially my own name and those of our children, my family members, and other prominent people that had made an impression on Curtis over the years.

"So, tell me again why you write down all those names?" I asked one day when Curtis had his notebook out and was writing in it.

"I have to give credit to the people I see during the day or that I've dreamed about that I feel are trying to help us, or people who I feel will play some kind of role in our life."

"Give credit? But how would anyone besides yourself know that the names are being written down?" I wondered.

"My journal is being read," was his answer.

"When? And by whom?" I asked, startled.

"Have you noticed that I leave my drawer open a little bit where I keep my journal? I set it up so that I can tell if anything has been moved, and it's been messed with."

"What? You think someone comes in our house while we're gone and reads your journal?" This was freaking me out.

"Don't worry," Curtis said. "They just want to see my journal, nothing else." I had occasionally peeked in his journal, curiosity getting the better of me, and I couldn't quite believe anyone would desire to read more than one entry. The journal entries were so vague that it was difficult to even guess what might be meant by them. They went something like, "A person with vindictive accusations caught being careless, ascertained as having ulterior motives, cannot be trusted" or "Prepare for 'snake' to rear its ugly head, increased discernment necessary."

And the name writing was enough to confuse anyone.

"I saw someone today that I haven't seen in a long time," Curtis would tell me. "The thing is, I just wrote their name in my journal three days ago." His tone of voice inferred that it wasn't a coincidence; it meant something.

"Well, if you write enough names of people you know, you are bound to run into one of them," I ribbed with a smirk.

"Sometimes I haven't seen them in years!" he exclaimed. "And then I see them within *days* of writing their name down? It's not just a coincidence. There's something to it," he insisted.

***

That following Monday, the 2010–2011 school year began. Chandy was living at home, trying to decide what to do next with her life. She had her bachelor's degree in psychology from Southern Utah University but couldn't find any work in her field of study. Some of her friends were going to China as youth ambassadors, which she thought sounded interesting, so she began to plan for that.

Levi was in his first year of college, Tyler was in tenth grade, and Mariah was in eighth. Steven lived at home but wasn't interested in attending college, so he spent his days working at Little Caesar's Pizza and playing World of Warcraft.

I could feel things shifting and changing in the family—three children who had graduated and only two children in secondary school—but the house still felt busy and active since all five children were living at home. Meals were big, shopping was still a major expedition, and, as usual, we had plenty of bills that needed to be paid, but for the first time in our lives, we were falling behind. Without the money we had brought in with fostering, with my cleaning jobs being cut to nearly a fourth of what they had been because the families I cleaned for were also hurting, and with Curtis not working any type of second job like he had nearly the whole time we'd been married, our income was cut in half. The downturn in the economy affected nearly everyone we knew, and it looked like we were going to lose our home. We were working with a short-sale specialist so we wouldn't have a foreclosure on our record, but the process was slow, and in the mean time, we paid all our bills like we always had, except our mortgage.

Turned out the mortgage would be the least of our worries.

8

"The ache for home lives in all of us, the safe place where we can go as we are and not be questioned." —Maya Angelou

THE PHONE RANG. CURTIS SAID IF IT WAS FOR HIM, HE wouldn't talk. That was strange. I knew Curtis didn't like talking on the phone that much, but he'd never outright refused to take a call.

The phone was rarely for him, but this time it was. "Hang on a minute," I said into the phone. Curtis was shaking his head emphatically and had a desperate, almost angry look on his face. I didn't know why he was so adamant about not talking, but I could tell he wouldn't budge.

"Curtis can't come to the phone right now," I said as truthfully as possible.

"This is Tony." Tony was Curtis's supervisor at the school. "Tell Curtis when he comes to work tomorrow to bring the letter with him, signed."

"What letter?" I asked.

"He'll know what I'm talking about. Just tell him."

"Okay, bye." I related the message to Curtis.

"There is no letter," he told me.

"Then why did he say there was?" I asked.

"He's just trying to stir up trouble," Curtis answered.

"Why didn't you want to talk on the phone?" I asked. I knew he hadn't always gotten along with Tony, but he'd never avoided his phone calls before.

"I'm not supposed to talk on the phone," Curtis explained. "To anyone."

"Why not?" I questioned further.

"I'm just not."

The next day I was busy doing my morning chores when Curtis walked in the door only an hour or so after he had left for work that morning. I stopped what I was doing, confused. This had never happened before in the twenty-one years Curtis had worked for the school district.

"What are you doing home?" I asked.

He smiled. He actually *smiled*. Then he just shrugged. "Who knows?" he answered.

I couldn't even begin to imagine what *that* meant.

"What do you mean, 'who knows'?" I asked.

"Who knows?" he said again.

He changed out of his work shirt and sat in the red chair with his vitamin supplement book. I was incredulous and didn't know what to think, so I did the only thing I knew how to do. I went back to my chores.

Then the phone rang. Curtis motioned wildly that he could not and would not talk on the phone. I recognized the principal's voice right away.

"Can I speak with Curtis?" he asked.

"He can't come to the phone right now." It felt like such a stupid thing to say because I knew he knew Curtis was home but just *wouldn't* come to the phone.

"Is this Pauline?"

"Yes."

"Pauline, would you let Curtis know he can come in and talk to me? I'm more than willing to talk with him. I know we can work this out if he'll just come in and have a chat with me."

This sounded bad. Like trying to talk a jumper off a ledge.

"I'll let him know," I stated as calmly as possible.

Curtis had always been extremely dedicated to his job. A job meant security for his family and his family meant everything to him, so, in my mind, whatever had gone wrong at the school could surely be rectified, and I was sure Curtis would do what he could to make things right.

"That was the principal," I said after I hung up. "He said you should go in and talk to him."

"I'm not supposed to," Curtis replied.

"Like you're not *supposed* to talk on the phone?" I asked with some sarcasm.

"Believe me, I'm not supposed to go in and talk to anyone *or* talk on the phone."

"So I'm supposed to put off anyone who calls?" I was getting a bit annoyed.

"Just don't answer the phone," he stated with a shrug.

I was still confused, but things were adding up just a bit—the call from Tony, this call, Curtis's strange actions. "Do you still have a job?" I asked, a touch of horror tingeing my voice.

"Don't worry. I have everything under control." Curtis was stubborn and had a mind of his own. I knew when I could manipulate a situation and when it was completely out of my league. This one was the latter.

It was strange having Curtis home all day every day. I knew I couldn't go in to his work to look for explanations because if Curtis found out I'd done that, I'd never hear the end of it from him. When he told me he had a situation under control, he meant it, and I was not to meddle.

I knew something wasn't right, but I couldn't fathom what to do about it. Nothing like this had ever happened in the twenty-four years we'd been married. I did worry, though, but I did that privately since Curtis wouldn't explain anything to me.

It occurred to me then that I had taken for granted how hardworking Curtis was. I had never needed to worry about him finding work or going to work before, and, now that I did, I realized how unsettling it was.

A week later, we received a letter in the mail stating the necessary actions Curtis would have to take if he wanted to keep his job. Curtis refused to even look at the letter. Again, he wasn't *supposed* to. He told me not to open anything from the school district. The realization hit me then that my husband was most likely going to get fired, and he wasn't going to do anything about it. Panic set in. What about the finances? How would we survive on just my paycheck?

"You're being fired?" I asked.

"I'm not being fired. They're just making it look like I am. Remember that dream I had about the principals?"

"Where you thought you would someday be the head custodian?"

Curtis nodded. "That's all it is, but there's so many politics and semantics involved in management. It's a game they have to play to make sure there's no angry employees that think they were supposed to get the job."

I couldn't argue with that because I had never gotten involved with anything at his work. I didn't know what went on once he left the house for work each day, beyond the small tidbits he shared with me, so for all I knew there truly was some type of promotion in the works, just like he said.

I found out later that it was all a line he was feeding me to placate me.

Things became clear when we received a letter from the superintendent stating the course of action the district was taking with Curtis and that if he had any objections about the declared proceedings, they needed to be in writing and submitted before September 27, 2010. He was being fired from the district for insubordination—for hiding in closets.

"You're going to do something about this, aren't you?" I asked Curtis after explaining to him the content of the letter.

"I don't have to. It's all being taken of," he explained.

"What's that supposed to mean?" I demanded.

"Just what I said. It's all being taken care of." He lowered his voice and spoke slowly. "I have a group of people pulling for me, and they're the ones who are going to take care of it."

"You mean like the AFT or something?" Curtis was a member of the American Federation of Teachers.

"Yeah, something like that," he said evasively.

I could tell that was all I was going to get out of him, so I figuratively threw up my hands and carried on. It became a waiting game. The letter had given a specific date, and Curtis had told me that a group of people was pulling for him, so the only thing I could do was wait and try to ignore the fact that our savings were being depleted.

9

"Trust and belief are two prime considerations. You must not allow yourself to be opinionated." —James Dean

W E LIVED FROM ONE DAY TO THE NEXT, SEEING what would happen. I wanted to trust Curtis when he told me there was a group pulling for him and they were taking care of everything, but somewhere inside I knew that wasn't the case. Weeks had gone by since we'd received the letter from the superintendent, and as far as I could tell, nothing was happening to rectify the situation, nor was Curtis making any moves to do anything about it.

Once I had accepted that Curtis would not be going back to the school for employment, I began to wonder if something had finally gotten to him at work and if he was just ready for a change. He'd worked for the district for twenty-one years, and I can only imagine how monotonous cleaning up after a bunch of teenagers would get after that many years, so I began my line of questioning again.

"So, what kind of job do you think you'll look for now?" I asked him one day. "The options are wide open. You can finally try something new."

"I'm not supposed to look for another job right now," Curtis replied.

"Well, I think we both know that you won't be going back to the school to work," I stated, letting him know in no uncertain terms that I knew his "everything is being taken care of" bit was hogwash. "This obviously means you'll be seeking for new employment, correct?"

"Like I said, I won't be looking for a job anytime soon." He barely glanced up at me from his supplement book when he said this, as if the whole conversation wasn't even worth his time. But to me it was a big deal. A huge deal. Our future was on the line. We had a family to take care of, and I certainly didn't want to end up in the streets, destitute and penniless.

"You can't be serious," I said in confusion. "Our savings isn't going to hold out. What do you expect us to live on?"

"Don't worry. Everything is being taken care of," he stated again.

"Not that I can see," I replied.

"Trust me," Curtis said.

If I had a dollar for every time he uttered that phrase . . .

"That's not good enough," I spat out. "Not this time. You've got to give me more to go on than a simple 'trust me.' I deserve more than that."

"Okay, okay," he said, finally putting his book down and turning his attention toward me. "I need to give The Game a chance to wrap itself up. I really feel like something will happen by Christmas, but to be certain, I want to give it until spring break."

No, not The Game again! I silently screamed in my head. Out loud I said, "So rather than looking for more work, you're willing to take the chance on something so unreliable?"

He didn't even bother to answer my question, which said to me that that's how it was going to be whether I liked it or not. I wasn't finished, though.

"You really won't be looking for a job until *spring break*?" I emphasized the last two words, anger lacing my voice. I knew our savings wouldn't hold out, or if it did, we would be pretty much broke by then. "How about November?" I begged, thinking we wouldn't be too bad off if we went another couple of months, but he wouldn't budge.

Early in September I was ready to insist he do something other than sit in his red chair all day, studying herbs and scratching down names, but then one night, *I* had a dream. And this wasn't just any dream.

I dreamed I was in a big house. It was empty and ugly. Not ugly like The Box, but still, it was plain and square. The room I was in was two stories high, with windows that helped light up the space. Plain square windows with no curtains or blinds. The walls of the house were painted a dull light blue, and there were piles of construction trash in the corners. It looked as though a renovation were in progress.

As I entered the house, I looked around and suddenly found myself flying through the air, weightless and not a bit scared. As I flew toward one wall, I could see that it would be necessary for me to do a flip and turn, like Olympic swimmers do when they reach the end of the pool and have to flip around and swim the other way. As I flipped and turned, the thought came to me, "I need to turn over a new leaf."

I couldn't imagine how it was possible that I was flying, but then another thought came to me: "Anything is possible."

I woke up with a surreal feeling surrounding me. The phrase *anything is possible* was all too familiar because that's what Curtis had believed his first dream had meant, and he had regularly repeated it. Although it was an odd sort of dream in an odd setting, it seemed significant.

Curtis asked me that morning if I'd had any dreams. He'd asked that off and on through the years, hoping, I think, that I would experience something that would make me a believer.

"Yes," I answered with a smile.

"What was it?" he asked eagerly. I proceeded to tell him about my dream.

Curtis laughed in relief, knowing that we would work together as a team now to win The Game—or end it, from my perspective. Whether or not I understood the hows or whys of what Curtis thought was happening, I'd had my first personal experience, and now it was time to move forward with faith.

I didn't believe in The Game any more than before, but I had the distinct feeling that the only way out of The Game was to play to the bitter end.

Little did I know how severely the vow I had just made would be tested.

***

With my newfound faith and determination, I listened intently when my husband told me anything about The Game, and rather than refusing to believe him or asking cynical questions, I calmly requested more details. He could hear in my voice that I was ready and willing to listen, and, in turn, he began to open up. My husband was still in the habit of speaking in vague terms, but I soon discovered how easy it was to encourage more information. He wanted so badly to talk about The Game because he felt that if he talked about it, he showed faith, and we would win in the end.

Much later I realized that my dream happened for a reason, and that it was ultimately our salvation. Without it and how it helped my husband open up, I may have never gotten enough information to put all the pieces of the puzzle together.

***

The ins and outs of The Game were explained to me time and time again, along with the criteria we were supposed to follow and the rewards of following that criteria. We often discussed what the rewards would be if we could be strict. Through the years, Curtis had shared a few of the details of The Game with me, but this would be the first time he explained everything. Luckily, he didn't find a need to only speak about The Game outside our home, and we were able to sit in the living room, he in his red chair and me on the couch, and talk. The kids, as usual, were out with friends.

"There's an individual who started this game," Curtis began, "that said he wanted to put us through a test to see if we would pass."

"Who is he, and why would he want to put us through a test in the first place?" I asked.

"He's a man of great influence in the community, and he considered that we were an upwardly mobile couple. He wanted me to be on his team, and he wanted to have influence with me."

"What do you mean, 'team'?"

"It's kind of a loose-knit team—political, religious. He wanted to gather people under his banner. He also wanted some gratuity."

"Gratuity?"

"Whatever this game brings in, whatever investments it brings in, he wanted a piece of the pie."

"But how did you figure out he had set up this test for us?" I asked.

"I felt like it was him. I had a dream about him one night. He looked just like one of the actors in a psycho movie, and that's just what he is, a psycho. He's always given me the cold chills whenever I'm around him.

"This 'originator' or 'orchestrator' called it a natural test—tests in natural settings to see how we would react, and he believed that if someone was watched closely or listened to, it wouldn't have any affect on them, it wouldn't change the way they did things, and they wouldn't have physical or mental changes come over them. Of course he was wrong, because it would affect them, but that's how psycho he was."

"When was this?" I asked.

"Back in 1994, when I was thirty years old. That's when I gained forty-five pounds. I had been the same weight for twelve years. And suddenly I would walk in a room and forget why I was there. I'd never done that before."

"So you think this started clear back in '94?"

"Late August of '94," Curtis replied. "It was after I'd had some dental work done."

"Does the dental work have to do with anything?" I inquired.

"Well, I came home more agitated. After that, it seems like I started to be more critical and negative about everything."

"It does seem like it was about that time that things got more difficult in our marriage," I agreed.

"Anyway, this originator would watch us through other people. Groups began to form. I began to notice that the shirts people wore had to do with what type of group they were in. Some were supportive of us as a couple; others would do anything to wreck our marriage for the chance to be with me. The same happened to you with men who wanted to be with you."

I had always hated it when he talked about all the men he thought were after me. I hadn't seen any evidence to support that except for Hank, but Curtis had told me these suspicions a few times through the years.

I rolled my eyes and motioned for him to go on. "You mentioned some groups that were forming?"

"Ohhhh . . . like, what's that company called, those popular shirt companies? If the shirt was white, it was better than red. That's what the people who had some of the more ulterior motives wore."

"Any other groups?" I asked.

"Yeah, some of the other main companies with logos on the shirts. But with any group, white was always the best color. Red and black were the worst. Hair color made a difference."

"What about hair color?"

"Blondes against the brunettes against the redheads," said Curtis.

"Against? What do you mean, 'against'?"

"There's a point system. Points come with energy. However much energy or money these people put into The Game is how much information they could gather. If they didn't put very much in, they got just the basics: height, weight, basic information. They needed to know who to promote so they would win bigger. It was like gambling—they could lose money on people or make money. Whoever I would be interested in would be the type they would want to promote, so they wanted to find out what types of qualities and characteristics I like. There might be someone in The Game who has someone else with them, like a young lady might have a non-partial boy with her. They would come up to me and take note of how enthusiastically I said hi. It was very well organized."

"So, if I'm understanding this right, the more someone invests, the more information they are given as to the type of person you would like? But what do they do with that information?"

"It's used for part of the test we are being put through, which is a test to see if we will remain together no matter what is done to separate us. But to make The Game more interesting, and to give ways for more people to be involved, I've discovered that at the very end, there will be a stage setting. I picture ten women coming out at the same time. The first ten will be blondes, then brunettes, then redheads. I'll have to eliminate five from each group."

"And why are they coming out on the stage?" I asked.

"There needed to be a way for people to win something. To create more interest in The Game, the orchestrator created this stage scene where everyone will be presented that has invested or has been promoted or sponsored. I have to narrow it down to the top three women I would choose as the most desirable, and they'll win a portion of the investments. Do you want to know who my top three would be?"

"Well, no, not really, but I bet I can guess at least one of them. She's a redhead, right?" I said. Curtis had always had a thing for redheads.

"Yes, she would be my number-one pick. She's a good person, and I know she's been through a divorce. If she showed up with the redheads, I would know that that group wasn't trying to separate us. They had good intentions toward us as a couple and weren't trying to get between us, so anyone in that group would be a good choice. The only reason any of this particular group would have any interest in me is if I outlived you or we got a divorce."

"So I take it the redheads have a pretty good chance on the stage."

"They do. Especially against the blondes. They represent being young and spoiled and unrealistic."

"All blondes, then?"

"The ones who acted that way created the whole stigma for the rest of the blondes."

I nodded for him to go on.

"I have to eliminate five from each group of ten, then those groups of five will be combined to make a new group of ten. Eventually, the redheads will probably dominate, since they're the best group going in."

"And I'll be involved too, you said?"

"Yeah, the same thing will happen in your case. I don't know who you should choose for the top picks, but I do know who needs to be at the bottom." Curtis then proceeded to list five men whom he strongly suggested be at the very bottom.

I rolled my eyes again. This wasn't something I could picture would ever take place, but for the sake of understanding where he was coming from and showing my support to him as a person, I listened to him and continued to ask questions.

"When do you think this will take place?" I asked.

"This game is twenty years long. It's like a retirement—you're tested for twenty years and you're done. It will be over in August of 2014."

That seemed so far away. He had promised he would start looking for a job by spring break, though, so I still planned to hold him to that.

***

On long walks, our clasped hands swinging between us, we continued to talk and talk about The Game, and the money, and all of the things we could use it for.

Curtis had been so vague previously anytime he mentioned anything involving The Game—names were never given, people were only hinted at—but he must have felt comfortable sharing more because now he started giving me examples, ways he was being tested.

"I was talking to a gentleman on the board of the condo complex where I did yard maintenance," Curtis explained. "He had bad eyes. I looked up and a lady came out on her balcony, nine o'clock in the morning, stark naked, and laid some things over the railing. I mentioned this to the man I was talking to. He glanced over and adjusted his glasses, then said, 'She's a beautiful woman.'

"Another time, there was an older man who came to me and said he wanted an oleander shaped a little differently. He had his back to the bush while I was facing the window. There was a sheer curtain at the window, and when I looked up, there was this man's wife in a robe. She proceeded to drop her robe and place her hands on her hips as if posing. This was a test to see if I would treat her any differently, act like I was interested in her. If not, I would prove my loyalty to you.

"There was a lady who kept trying to get me to fix her shower too. She was probably thirty. She was in her swimming suit, and admittedly she was thin, had a nice face. She said, 'Just look at my shower. See what you think.' She repeated this over a week or two, very persistently, and most of the time she was wearing her swimming suit because she spent a lot of time at the pool. I looked at her shower but couldn't see anything wrong with it. Just the vibes from her made me think she wanted me to shower with her.

"Then there was the woman who tried to get me to fix her clogged dryer vent. She was about thirty also, and when she approached me, she was in a skimpy bikini. She said, 'Can you just come in my house and look at it?' She looked like she'd had a boob job, looked as though she could be in the Sports Illustrated Swimsuit Issue, and acted as though she was trying to lure me inside. I didn't go inside. I told her it wasn't my job to look at dryer vents.

"I just felt like I was being tested with all these setups. These would be reported by the people trying to lure me in if I were to fall into any of their traps."

I was speechless. I couldn't imagine why Curtis would make up such stories, but to believe them was a bit of a stretch. I wasn't going to call him a liar, so I said something like, "How strange," and left it at that.

***

Day after day, Curtis continued to pour out information I had previously been unaware of.

"The days leading up to my last day of work were really hard for me," Curtis revealed. "I'm glad I'm not working right now. It would have been way too difficult."

"What do you mean?" I asked. "Were you given a difficult route for this year?" The custodians rotated sections of the school that they were in charge of, so each year they had a new routine.

"It didn't have anything to do with my routine. It had to do with the people at the school," Curtis answered.

"What people?" I asked.

"Everyone. I used to be able to tell between the people for us or against us, but it became harder and harder to tell. I'm not supposed to talk to anyone who's against us or it will give them points, so when I couldn't tell as easily who was okay to talk to, I just stopped talking to everyone."

A light went on in my mind as I remembered my conversation with Mary the previous school year, just before summer. "You really didn't talk to anyone?" I asked in surprise. It was a big school. "Sometimes it's necessary to communicate with your coworkers and your supervisor, so how did you get around that?"

"I just gestured and nodded or shook my head," he answered with a smile.

"You're kidding." I remarked, dumbfounded.

"And, like, whenever one of the students would say something to me, at first I would nod my head their way and give them a high-five, but it got too hard not to say anything, so I started walking around with my head down, so I wouldn't catch anyone's eye."

"How awkward!" I said.

"It was. I'm just glad I'm not still working there."

I didn't know whether to feel compassion for his predicament or bewilderment that he would actually go to such extremes.

Then out of the blue one day, Curtis struck up a conversation.

"It was from heaven."

"What was?" I asked.

"That first dream. It wasn't ten, it was a hundred times more powerful than anything I've ever experienced. Shortly after that, I wrote down two names of people that I wanted to help, once we had the means to help them. One of them was a cousin of mine. I left her name in plain view, and within weeks, *weeks* of writing her name down, she took her own life."

"I remember you saying something about that," I said.

"I always attributed her suicide to the fact that she was being watched." *Whoa, this was news to me.* "They pushed her over the edge with their negative comments, with the way they intruded in her life through the players of The Game.

"Wait, hold on," I said. "How was she suddenly involved in The Game just because you wrote her name down?"

"They watched her because they're interested in who I'm interested in."

"How did anyone know you had written down her name?" I asked.

"Don't you remember? We were told to leave the door unlocked so that a package could be delivered. It took three weeks for that package to get to us. Someone could have easily come in during that time and saw the notebook I had written her name on." He shook his head in sorrow. "I had such a strong feeling that I would eventually be able to help her. It was so powerful, I remember not believing at first that she was dead."

I remembered that day very clearly. I was aghast that he would think his cousin's death had been faked, that someone was pulling a huge prank. "People don't do that," I had told him. "They wouldn't fake someone committing suicide." It wasn't until we found the eulogy in the newspaper my husband finally conceded that it had to be true.

But I hadn't realized until now that in Curtis's mind, his cousin's death was tied to The Game.

As the days went by, he would talk longer and longer, sometimes bringing up things from the past that he had kept to himself, other times speaking with a bit of urgency when he mentioned the actions that would be required of us—like staying away from certain numbers, as I soon learned about, or like not talking to the wrong people so they wouldn't get points—the consequences of which I never would have or could have guessed.

10

"What you focus on with your thought and feeling is what you attract into your experience." —*The Secret*

AS TIME PROGRESSED, THE GAME RULED EVERY waking moment. The rituals were set. The rules were specific. There was no turning back this time.

We began a shopping ritual every Friday morning. My husband would climb out of the van at each of our stops, wait for me to reach his side, and then hold out his right hand for me to grasp. I always had to be on his right side, sit on his right at the movies, walk on his right. After a while, I became accustomed to it, and it felt strange if I was on his left. I didn't know at the time why he always wanted me on the right—just that he was insistent about it.

Sometime in September, shopping took on a whole new twist. You've heard of paint by number? This was life by number. Looking back, it may have been my fault that numbers began to mean so much. Or maybe we can just blame it on Wendy's.

To backtrack, I had been cleaning homes since 2004, and on the days that I cleaned, I would often need to stop and grab something for lunch. Wendy's was one of my favorite places to stop, and I usually ordered off the dollar menu. This particular time, however, I was craving a larger-than-value-sized chocolate Frosty, so I ordered a medium, plus a Jr. Cheeseburger Deluxe, a value fry, and a five-piece chicken nuggets. I usually only got two or three items, but I must have been famished that day. When I got my order, they had given me a value Frosty and a medium fry instead of the other way around. Not a big deal, so I didn't ask them to change it, but when I looked at the receipt, it just seemed unusual that it came to exactly $4.44. Four had always been my favorite number, so a triple four was especially good—or so I thought.

Curtis was often looking for clues—anything that might help him understand better what was happening with The Game—and he'd always had a fascination with numbers, so when I told him about my day, off-handedly mentioning the Wendy's receipt, he immediately began wondering if there was anything significant to it. I knew he loved numbers because he knew many of the world records from the Guinness book by heart, and he could add figures as fast as he could say them, but his new fascination was forming on a totally different level.

Suddenly, the law of attraction began to play a prominent role in our lives. The number 4 was everywhere! I'd wake in the night, 4:44 a.m. Curtis would glance at the clock in the afternoon, 4:44 p.m. License plates, numbers on jerseys , prices of items on the end caps at Walmart, random papers stuck to the floor in Home Depot. It felt strange and intrusive, and even I began to wonder if it meant something. But was it lucky . . . or unlucky? Or neither?

Years went by with continued occurrences of the number 4. We spent spring break of 2007 in Mesa, Arizona, at my sister's house because it was an inexpensive vacation and gave us a chance to see family. I have a brother, Robert, in Mesa too. He came to visit one evening, and my sister needed something at a neighbor's house, but it was a bit too far to walk. Robert offered to let me check out his new Toyota Prius. It was the first time I had ever driven it, and it was pretty cool to check out all the bells and whistles he had added as upgrades. Then I looked at his mileage.

44,444 miles. No joke.

Our trip was so short that even when we returned to Steph's house, it still read 44,444. I was beside myself. What could this mean? How bizarre was this that I would just happen to drive his car right at that time when I had never driven it before or since?

We took a long-awaited trip to Disneyland for spring break in March 2009, which we'd saved for nearly a year for. On our way home, we stopped in Primm, Nevada, on the state line to grab a bite to eat. It would seem everyone else had the same idea that we did; get out of the busy part of California, then find a place to stop. We finally found a place to park and went into McDonald's to order. I looked at my receipt. We were customer number 444.

This number obsession went on for nearly six years, but it had increased in intensity by the fall of 2010. Without my knowledge, certain numbers had taken on meanings in The Game.

"How many places do you have on your list?" my husband asked me one Friday in September. It was shopping day, plus we ran other errands that needed to be taken care of.

I counted the places I needed to go: bank, library, bread store, dollar store, Walmart, and Costco. "Six," I told him.

"Cut one out," he said.

"Why?" I asked.

"Because we're not supposed to go to six places."

Curtis insisted that we go to three or five places, including any place he needed to go; never four, six, seven, or eight, which were bad numbers according to The Game. He told me that they had been "bought up" by the players of The Game, by people with ulterior motives. If we did something that involved those numbers, the wrong people would get points. All this time that I had wondered what all the 4s meant, whether they might be lucky or unlucky, Curtis already knew.

"How did you figure all this out?" I wondered.

"I asked," Curtis said.

"How could anyone possibly know what numbers we use or don't use?" I wondered. It was something I genuinely could not fathom.

"I have to report," he stated in a matter of fact tone.

"Report to who?" I asked.

"To the orchestrators of The Game." He wouldn't give me more of an explanation than that.

He never left the house alone, and we never talked to anyone about The Game when we were out and about, so I couldn't imagine when he reported anything to anyone—except for when he went to the gas station a few blocks down the road to fill a tire that leaked on the van.

He began parking the van on the street in front of our house, so I asked him what he was doing. He told me that someone was letting air out of the tire so that he would have to go to the gas station. That's where he reported to someone about The Game, he said, so he wanted the person to have easy access to the tire to let out the air. Then he would know when he needed to go report.

I refused to let this continue. The cul-de-sac was used for a soccer field at night, with twenty-eight kids spread between the four families that lived there. They needed plenty of space to play.

Curtis insisted we follow his number system, however, even though it was inconvenient. If there were four places we needed to go on shopping day, I had to eliminate one. We could only shop from 9:00 a.m. to 12:00 p.m. because my husband said that was the only time we had protection while we were away from home—that and date night. We couldn't buy items with bad numbers in their prices. I would slip something into the cart and glance at my husband. He'd shake or nod his head. Sometimes I would comply, and other times I would be assertive and keep what I had chosen. I had to purchase one, three, or five of any particular item: bags of chips, packs of hot dogs, cans of soup, and so on. We had to go to checkout stands with only good numbers, regardless of whether shorter lines were available.

My husband counted the number of items in our grocery cart to be sure it wasn't a bad number. We had the dreaded forty-four items once, but we didn't realize it until we were in the checkout line. Curtis quickly threw a pack of gum on the belt and sighed in relief.

We exited the grocery store one day, and as my husband looked over the receipt, he glanced at me in horror. The bill had come to $44.46. This was not acceptable. My husband fretted about it all the way home. Then, as we were unloading the groceries, he hauled the new weights he had bought into the house (now that he couldn't work out at the gym at the school, he needed something he could work out with at home). He checked the price of each weight on the receipt and stated, "I'll just take back one of these five pounders. I didn't need it anyway. Then that will fix everything."

Curtis would discipline himself to sit in his red chair during certain hours of the day. From 7:00 to 9:00 a.m., he would remain locked in his red recliner, either reading or just thinking, and then from 9:00 a.m. to 10:00 a.m. he would get up and move about. He would start a load of laundry at that time. He'd have a bite to eat and use the restroom. Then from 10:00 to 11:00 it was back in the red chair. Noon to 1:00, 2:00 to 3:00, 4:00 until 5:00. He kept up this ritual with exactness. The evening hours were free hours. It was only during the day that he subjected himself to chair duty.

"Why do you feel like you need to keep that type of schedule?" I asked him one day.

"Because of the bad numbers," he explained once again. "Besides, it gives me time to think. I need time to think. That's how I know what needs to happen next. That's how I know where my disciplines need to be."

***

The heat of summer didn't give way to cooler fall temperatures until mid-October, so in September, the days were still plenty hot enough to need air conditioning. Always wanting to save money wherever possible, I kept the thermostat on eighty degrees and turned it up to eighty-two when no one would be home all day. My husband needed cooler temperatures to sleep well at night, so seventy-eight degrees was agreed upon for the night setting, then each morning I would turn it up for the day. At one point, I began to notice the air was coming on a lot more than usual during the day, so I checked the thermostat. It was on seventy-eight, so I keyed it up to eighty. Later the same day, I checked again and noticed that it was again set to seventy-eight, so I turned it back up. After a couple of days of this, I decided to question Curtis, since, besides me, he was the only other person who could have adjusted the temperature.

"Why do you keep turning down the temperature during the day?" I asked.

"It's supposed to be at seventy-eight," he replied matter-of-factly.

"That's only what we keep it on at night. You know I like to keep it higher during the day." I was a bit miffed because now, of all times, we needed to save money anywhere we could.

"Believe me, it's *supposed* to be on seventy-eight," he restated.

"Why?" I asked, not letting this one go.

"If you take the letters of the alphabet and put a number with each letter, like *A* is one, *B* is two, et cetera, the letters of your name add up to seventy-eight." He then mentioned that a woman of questionable character and motives in The Game had letters in her name that added up to eighty, so he insisted that from then on, I needed to leave the thermostat on seventy-eight. At times like this, I wanted to ask how he expected to be able to pay the higher electric bill, but then I knew what his answer would be. We would have plenty of money when we won The Game.

After hearing his explanation about the temperature, I discovered a wad of folded index cards. My husband used a lot of index cards to write down his discoveries from his vitamin book, so it was common to see them strewn about the house. These particular ones, though, had words with a series of numbers written under them. The strange format made me take a second look.

Valor Hall 22-23-35-50-68 8-9-21-33
Exercise 5-29-34-52-55-64-83-88

Walking 23-24-36-47-56-70-77
Jogging 11-26-33-40-49-63-70

I was mesmerized—and somewhat horrified. I somehow knew this strange code was a code that my husband lived by. Flashes of memories began pounding through my head. Times when my husband would tell me to be cautious of someone or something, like the people I cleaned for or the school where I worked. No way could he have known what type of people I worked with, but his precautionary urgencies spoke otherwise. He had also set up a sort of rehab schedule after I broke my leg. "Go one mile today, wait a day, then go two miles." He had laid out a plan for weeks at a time. There was more:

Milk 13-22-34-45
Salsa 19-20-32-51-52
Almond 1-13-26-41-54-58
Rice 18-27-30-33
Soy 19-34-59

More memories. For a while, my husband insisted on drinking only soy milk. He said it was because dairy milk made his joints hurt. He had also tried rice milk and almond milk and ate rice nearly every meal for probably two months straight or longer. He ate rice with hot dogs, salad, tomato soup or cream of chicken soup or chicken noodle soup, rice with barbecue sauce, rice with tomato sauce. He ate it constantly. He always had strange disciplines like that, and he'd always tell me it was because of some health or vitamin reason. The list went on:

Oatmeal 15-16-36-49-54-55-67
Chicken 3-11-20-23-34-39-53
Noodle 14-29-44-48-60-65
Butter 2-23-43-63-68-86
Margarine 13-14-32-39-40-58-67-81-86
Macaroni (8) 13-14-17-18-36-51-65-74
Tomato (6) 20-35-48-49-69-84
Watermelon (10) 23-24-44-49-67-80-85-97-112-126

And on and on: Monday, Tuesday, Wednesday, Thursday, Friday, Saturday, Sunday, beef, bean, vacuum, spoon, fork, knife, yogurt, lettuce, cabbage, piano, reading, bananas, sweeping, dishes, laundry, colors—blue, black, yellow—hair (with an X by the numbers for yellow), peanut butter, and eggs.

It wasn't completely clear how to read this code he had written, but observing what he'd done in his daily life, I could make some assumptions about what numbers were good and what numbers weren't. Laundry must have made the cut because my husband had been doing the laundry since before this all began.

Many times Curtis would show me a math problem he'd figured out and tie it in to The Game. He would use multiplication or addition, whatever worked, and would come up with dates—days, months, years—that he felt something big would happen: the big payout. There were other times when my husband would use numbers to help him with his predictions, like the year when I turned forty and Curtis turned forty-four, which was back in 2007. When nothing happened within that year, we heard over the television someone saying that Obama was the forty-fourth president of the United States. Suddenly, there was a new time frame for his predictions to come true, one that would last at least four years! Thank goodness he was only insisting on waiting until spring break (if he kept his word) to see if anything would happen. With circumstances as they were, and as they were about to become, no way could I have lasted another four years.

11

"Don't sweat the small stuff . . . and it's all small stuff." — *Richard Carlson*

OW THAT CURTIS HAD DISCOVERED A SYSTEM TO put a number on everything, more rules began to pop up. The colors of cars were a factor in decisions that my husband made, which wouldn't have made any sense to me except that I remembered there were colors listed on his index cards. He didn't know I had seen them, though, so I decided to question him a little.

"When did you start determining that certain colors were good and bad?"

"I asked," Curtis calmly replied.

"Asked who?" I said. I assumed he was saying that he asked the machine in the closet, but I decided to find out for sure.

"Another custodian," was his reply. Obviously, this had been before he was fired. This was new to me. Had he really spoken to another custodian about this?

"Which one?" I questioned. I knew quite a few of the custodians, from the stories my husband had told me through the years or meeting them at the annual Christmas party. Occasionally the turnover was pretty quick, though, so I didn't always know everyone—like this time.

"George. He's Mexican and doesn't speak a lot of English. I don't think you've met him yet."

"What did he say?" I pressed. "What exactly did you ask him?"

"I asked him if some colors are better than others, colors that people are wearing when they approach or walk by. He said yes."

It was such an odd question to ask someone that I didn't even know how to respond. I wondered if they had spoken about anything else involving The Game, but Curtis was so tight-lipped about it, even swearing *me* to secrecy, that I could hardly imagine he would have said anything else to George. He wasn't finished, though.

"Do you remember when I told you that I started to wonder who I could talk to and who I couldn't?" he asked.

"You mean when you said you didn't know who was for us or against us, so you didn't talk to anyone at the school?"

"Yeah. Once I learned about colors, I watched for patterns—the colors certain people wore, where they would stand. It was hard to keep it all straight, but I know color had something to do with who was for us and who was against us. Dark colors were bad, and white or light colors were good."

It seemed impossible to me that a whole school would be in on The Game and even more impossible that what the students wore to school was somehow connected, but as with everything else I had trouble understanding, I had to let it go and somehow trust that Curtis knew what he was talking about. That meant that now not only numbers but colors would affect our lives.

Curtis informed me that he had a system going in the garage. If there were things in the house that we owned that he felt were holding us back from making progress in The Game, he would place them just inside the garage, where they would await a verdict. He would then watch the vehicles in the cul-de-sac, and if a dark-colored vehicle showed up after he took something into the garage, he would know that he had made the right choice in taking it out of our house. That item needed to be removed from our home permanently. When light-colored cars entered the cul-de-sac, this was a good thing, and it meant that we could keep the item.

His method for determining if an item might qualify to be removed from our home and placed in the verdict pile in the garage (because it was holding us back from making progress in The Game) was threefold: (1) Its origin: did it come from someone that either had undesirable intentions toward us or didn't believe we were meant for each other, or did it come from somewhere that was now considered our opposition? (2) Its use: had it been used by someone who was a foe in The Game? (3) Who had touched it or influenced it in any way: had it been touched by someone from the wrong side?

I watched as other items in the house were sentenced. As I came around the corner from the kitchen to the living room, I caught Curtis standing in the doorway with the door open, holding up a can of tomato sauce. He shut the door, passed by me and into the garage, put the can into the verdict pile, and then returned to his red recliner, where he could see outside as the colors of cars acted as jury.

I had purchased the tomato sauce at the Harmon's case lot sale, but Steven worked at Walmart, so Curtis felt that we should only support Walmart now. That's why the can of tomato sauce went into the garage in the first place—he wanted to test his theory. Sure enough, after being tried and sentenced, it lost. We were now limited to shopping only at Walmart. Stores like the dollar store and the bread store were on my shopping list because I tried to shop with savvy and thrift, and Costco had always been a favorite place to shop. I dreaded buying hamburger anywhere else, so I told Curtis that we needed to stop there just for hamburger. Luckily, one was a good number, so he let me buy that one item at Costco.

We still went out on our Friday-night dates, although now, more often than not, we just picked up a movie from Redbox to watch at home. Our lower income required many such adjustments.

One evening we were driving to one of the Redboxes over in the Albertson's shopping center. We were alone in the van, so I asked my husband a question I had been wondering about, something that had to do with The Game.

Curtis glanced at the dashboard then over at me. He placed a finger to his lips and said, "Shhh," then pointed to the brake light. I shrugged in confusion. "I'll tell you later," he said.

Our van was built in the mid-nineties, so it had quirks that had begun to pop up with more frequency. One of those quirks was the tendency for the brake light to come on at any given time even though the emergency brake wasn't set.

When we got out of the van to go pick a movie, Curtis explained.

"Our van is bugged," he said. "Whenever the brake light is on, we need to be careful what we talk about because someone is listening."

I remembered my vow, so I nodded my head and agreed not to say anything revealing when the brake light was on.

***

The following week went by in a similar fashion. Items from the house would gradually end up in the garage to await their sentence. If the verdict was negative, they went into the massive pile in the center of the garage that we would later load into the van and take to the donation center. We had to remove both backseats from the van to fit everything in.

My dishes in the kitchen, the nice ones, were a casualty of The Game. One day they were just gone. I found out later that it was the name of the dinnerware that had caused them to be removed—a name too similar to an opposing player in The Game.

My only set of china would have to go because it was from my mother-in-law. Beautiful blue-and-white-patterned Currier and Ives china.

I decided not to sweat the small stuff.

It didn't stay small.

12

"If I won't be myself, who will?" —*Alfred Hitchcock*

OUR NEW TABLE HAS BEEN SACRIFICED TO THE GAME Gods. I had asked for Hank's advice when I went shopping for it because he had once been a salesman at a department store. He even showed up at the store while I was shopping. I didn't take his advice, and he never touched my table (it was shipped from overseas and took six months to arrive), but just the fact that he was in the vicinity while I was shopping for a table makes it "unkeepable." Some lucky buyer at the thrift store will get a seven-hundred-dollar table for one-fourth of that or less.

My sister is storing a glass patio table in our garage, so I pull it into the house and clean off all the cobwebs. I tape the hole in the middle where the umbrella post goes and duct tape the bottom of the metal legs so they won't scratch our wood laminate floor.

More and more items make their way unwillingly to the garage. There is an exodus of all sorts of items, from dishes to dressers, tarps to trampolines. It's like a beast we have to feed or it will devour us instead.

Curtis is anxious to get rid of as many things as possible, assuring me that in the long run, we'll get far more back than we ever gave away.

"They set everything that we donate aside," Curtis explains to me, "then they auction it off to the highest bidder. The more things we give, the more the pot will grow, so we win it back anyway."

"Why would anyone be interested enough in our stuff to actually bid on it and pay big money for it?" I ask in disbelief.

"Because we're people of importance," Curtis reminds me, as if for the hundredth time. His voice has taken on the tone of someone who's trying to explain something but you just don't get it. "There are people, a lot of people, that want to own something we used to own. Believe me, I know what I'm talking about," he adds when he sees me shaking my head no.

Regardless of my disbelief, he continues to evaluate all our possessions for removal purposes. "Didn't we get this couch from a single lady?" Curtis asks. I know where this is headed.

But I am living by faith, so out it goes into the garage, another sacrifice to The Game Gods. He takes an axe to two couches; the other one his mother gave us.

It wasn't barbarism, his use of an axe. It was simple logic. We don't have a vehicle large enough to haul a couch to the donation center, so he chops it up into small enough pieces to fit into our trash bins. If we tried to sell or give away our couches, people might start asking questions.

The kids begin to ask where everything is going, but I just shrug. "It's all just . . . gone."

My mother taught me well that people are more important than things, so although letting go is difficult, it isn't impossible. But soon, *people* are involved, not just things. And not just *any* people.

***

Chandy is in the kitchen making herself some breakfast and asks her dad why he chopped up the couches. He gives her a blank stare.

"Aren't you going to answer me?" Chandy asks.

"It depends on who you are today." After that, he doesn't speak to her anymore.

"Is there a reason you aren't speaking to Chandy?" I ask. Curtis is downstairs watching the news.

"One word: *proxy*. That's all I'm gonna say for right now," he replies.

But it isn't just Chandy. The signs have to blink neon before I discover what's going on. He is speaking to only one of our five children.

***

"Why do you only talk to Steven?" We're lying in bed that night.

"Proxy," he says again.

"Please elaborate," I quietly plead.

"You have to promise not to tell anyone this. They can't know that we know."

"Okay," I promise as I choke on the breath in my throat. He doesn't notice.

He stares intently at me, then lowers his voice and speaks slowly. "Our children, all except Steven, have taken on personalities by proxy. They all represent someone with ulterior motives, someone who isn't for us."

I hardly dare breathe for fear he won't continue. I need more information.

"Who?" I squeak.

"Mariah represents someone with the initials M. M. If I talk to her, the wrong people get points."

"How about the other kids?"

"They've taken on personalities of people who are against us, people that have the same hair color or the same initials. We can't talk to them because we don't want them to win."

This new discipline is so unfathomable that I am tempted to call ask-a-nurse or even my dad to ask why in the world Curtis would think such a thing. I wonder if there could possibly be an explanation for his actions, although I have no idea what that explanation might be. Curtis's actions are so odd that I find myself wanting to talk to someone about it, but, not wanting to break my promise of secrecy, I keep everything to myself.

We are all in the kitchen the next day, milling about, and I watch as Curtis spins and twirls every time he passes by Mariah.

Steven's time soon runs out too.

He pulls me into the garage and shuts the door. "Why isn't Dad talking to me anymore?" he asks.

"It's not something I can tell you," I explain sadly, "but just know that it doesn't have anything to do with you. Just be patient. Everything will be fine."

Steven is definitely the most sensitive of our children, and I feel horrible not being able to explain anything to him. Levi, on the other hand, is probably glad his dad isn't speaking to him.

Chandy is our most inquisitive child. She has questions about everything. "Why doesn't Dad talk to any of us kids?" "Why are you getting rid of the couches?" "Where did the table go?"

Again, I feel bad that there is so much I can't share with her, but I try to answer as truthfully as possible. "He's not speaking to any of you because he feels like he isn't supposed to right now. It won't last forever." "He feels like we aren't supposed to keep the couches." "The table is just . . . gone." I can't even begin to try to explain that one.

Nothing rattles Tyler, though, bless his heart, and Mariah is the same.

Their vast number of friends keeps them occupied and for the most part unaware of all the drama of The Game.

***

Although I am unable to tell my kids many things, I have free reign to talk to Curtis about The Game, and at times I have nearly as many questions as Chandy does.

"Why did you stop talking to Steven today?" I ask. I am calm. Just curious.

"When he was sitting on the couch, he turned his left shoulder outward," my husband answers.

"How does that mean anything?"

"I noticed something at the school. I'd pass by on the left of some girls, and the next time I walked past them, they'd be sitting up against the wall so that I couldn't pass on the left. It was like they were trying to make it so I had to pass on the right, but that would give the wrong people points, so I just turned and walked backward until I got past them."

"Seriously?" I ask.

"When I swept the halls, I swept to the left too," he adds.

"Why?" This made no sense.

"Because I'm supposed to," he answers. "I keep you and only you on my right, and everyone and everything else is left."

"That's why you spin whenever you pass by Mariah," I said with new understanding, though not comprehension.

When it comes time for Chandy to leave for China on September 27, Curtis doesn't even hug her good-bye at the airport. I cry when we're out of her sight.

My husband attempts to console me. "It's better that she'll be gone. That's one less person we have to avoid speaking to."

13

*"'Tis this desire of bending all things to our own purposes
which turns them into confusion and is the chief source of every
error in our lives."* —Sarah Fielding

T'S FRIDAY MORNING, OCTOBER 8, 2010. I DON'T HAVE
work on Fridays, so I'm home. The kids are at school, and Steven is still
asleep. I sit on blankets on the floor where the couch used to be, and
Curtis is sitting in the red chair. I try to reason with him. "Families talk
to each other," I plead as the tears start falling. "There's no way that God
or anyone else would require you to eliminate that from your life," I say in
my crying voice. I hear my breath catch on a high sob.

"It's only for a short time." My husband sits on the front edge of the
red chair and leans toward me, imploring me to understand. "We're being
tested, and it's got to be near the end of The Game since they're asking
something so difficult."

"Still, there's no possible way that anyone would require this of you,"
I insist.

"It is what it is, and we have to follow the rules. It's becoming harder
because the pot has grown so big." He lowers his voice and looks at me
with grave severity and says each word succinctly, "The pot is over *thirty-
three million dollars* now."

"I don't care about the money!" I cry. "You can't just not speak to our
children! They're hurting. They don't understand what's going on."

"They're fine—they aren't themselves," he explains. Always calm.
Always certain. "They know it's supposed to be this way, I promise. Just
hang in there a little while longer."

"How long!" I yell, as I bury my face in my hands and cry hard. I take
huge gasping breaths and rock back and forth.

"It can't be much longer. I feel like this has to be close to the end." He continues to offer reassurances. His calm voice settles me down. Somehow, in all the teary fog, I remember my resolve to have faith. To see this through. I feel like this is the hardest thing I've ever done in my life.

I nod my head and carry on. Things are always so serious now. I miss our laughter the most. It's just . . . gone. Like the couches and table.

We do our Friday shopping, same as usual. We take another load to the donation center. My husband's newest discipline: he doesn't speak to *anyone* . . . but me.

We have another long conversation again that night. Or, more accurately, he talks and I listen. He has bottled up so much for so long that it just comes spilling out, not always making sense to me.

"The only way to keep so many people interested in betting on The Game," Curtis explains, "was to tell them that it would be worth at least one million dollars to them if they got in, and the only way to keep The Game from ending was to double the pot. As long as the pot kept doubling, the orchestrators had incentive to keep The Game going. It got bigger than anyone imagined.

"It's a game of chance. People had to use their instincts to decide what they thought the payout would be and when to jump in and bet or maybe wait.

"Each player has the opportunity to win votes, just like we do, and their votes count toward our total if they're on our side. They're like our sponsors—the best ones would be the people you knew, and they would try to gather support and have people take a chance on them."

"If someone talks to others quite a bit that have a certain hair color or height, someone who's quiet or outgoing, the orchestrators try to find someone with similar attributes to be in the competition and maybe lead the players astray, which would bring increased interest—a lot of interest—from the people betting. It's a unique game that is habit forming."

The whole conversation is beginning to make my brain feel like mush. My husband doesn't need any encouragement, though, so he keeps talking.

"Because of that, because of the extreme interest in us, it brought about increased heaven and hell, blessings and curses, exponentially, because people would think and pray and scheme *for us* and *against us*.

"In the school system, there were climbers who were ridiculous. Even teachers, an unbelievable amount of teachers that were hired, were single."

Oh boy, I think. *Here we are, back at the single women thing.*

"I didn't look at things critically enough, so when I did, everyone around us became a suspect. It wasn't all bad. There were some good people that came into our life."

My head is spinning by now. I don't know how much longer I can keep up, or at least pretend to keep up. Sometimes I have a lot of questions and I probe my husband for answers, but other times I am just plain tired of The Game, and this is one of those times. Especially when I remember that my husband isn't speaking to any of our children.

14

"The difference between a house and a home is like the difference between a man and a woman—it might be embarrassing to explain, but it would be very unusual to get them confused." —Daniel Handler (as Lemony Snicket)

IT'S THE WEEKEND. THE YOUNGER KIDS ARE OUT WITH friends. Steven emerges from downstairs.

"Hi, Steven," I say. He's groggy and looking for food, so he doesn't say much.

My husband is sitting in the red chair. He refuses to acknowledge Steven. I sit on the blanket-couch and sob. My resolve to have faith and see this through is swallowed when I see my husband ignore the kids. He reassures me again that this will end soon.

***

Emails to and from Chandy in China become one of my only outlets. My messages to her are about the goings on at the school where I work or anything recent in the news, like the big hailstorm Phoenix got and the three tornadoes that touched down near Flagstaff—but never about what is *really* going on at home. Ironically, Chandy writes about my sister in one of her emails:

> Stephanie is awesome . . . her day-to-day life makes for some pretty funny stories—you should have a character like Stephanie in a book you write. You guys are quite different . . . she likes chaos and you like order.

Order? I feel like my life is anything but order, but Chandy knows very little of what is going on. She only knows that her dad has been fired and that he isn't speaking to any of the kids.

***

Monday, October 11, 2010

Dear Chandy,

Life is strange but good. I have a friend on Facebook that has a title for her blog, "Life in the Peanut Butter Lane." I wonder what I would call my life right now . . . "The Time in My Life When I Tried to See What I Was Taking for Granted and Appreciate It More" maybe, or "Twilight Saga: The Husband in the Red Chair." Funny, I will probably never look at that red chair the same again.

It's Monday. Time to read scriptures in the morning before school. Curtis is sitting in the red chair. I get the books out and he shakes his head. I'm not sure I understand. We always read scriptures together. I move toward the stairs to call to the kids. He grabs my hand as I walk by and says, "No scriptures. Think proxy."

We are forbidden to read scriptures with the proxy people. Curtis is now treating the kids as though they aren't even his children. He feels that the better he plays that role, the more successful he is at The Game. He asks me to do the same. He wants me to stop talking to my own children.

I'd rather die.

"How can anyone expect us to not speak to our children *and* not read scriptures together? This sounds like something that can't possibly be good or right," I tell him.

"There's good people involved and they're pulling for us, I promise" he answers. "If we can just hold out, the benefits will be so much greater than the sacrifice."

"It still doesn't sound right to me," I respond hotly. "It can't be, no matter what the payoff is." Still, he isn't budging. I need a new angle, a different approach. Something drastic.

I stew about it all day at work. Who knows how long this will go on, my husband not speaking to our children and not letting us read scriptures together? He has ceased to act like a father. As far as his children are concerned, he might be anybody. It feels hopeless—heartless. I want my husband back. I want the father of my children to return.

When I get home from work, I plead with my husband: "Please stop playing The Game! It's gotten out of control, and I don't want any part of it anymore."

"I've told you before. We can't stop. We have to see it through to the end," he explains. Still calm. Still certain.

"But can you at least talk to the kids and read scriptures with us?"

He shakes his head. "That's the criteria I have to follow. It is what it is. I have to follow the rules."

I try something desperate. "Then if you're going to take your heart out of the home, I'll take out mine!" I state fiercely. I then proceed to remove everything that makes a house a home. I take down every photo, every wall hanging, even the vinyl lettering on the walls: "Families that laugh together, last forever"; "Speak kind words and you will hear kind echoes"; "Live simply. Give more. Expect less." With all the loads we have taken to the donation center, the house looks really empty now. It echoes like a cavern.

The kids come in the house after school, and, seeing what I've been doing, they ask if we're moving. I promised the kids previously that we would let them know ahead of time if there was a move on the horizon, but now I probably look like a liar. Boxes are everywhere, packed with stuff from all over the house: fake plants, ceramic pieces, my wooden car collection, even the pictures of Jesus. I want to be thorough to see if it will jolt some sense into my husband.

He doesn't even bat an eye. He just sits calmly in his stupid red chair.

15

"But the cure for most obstacles is, Be decisive." —George Weinberg

I T'S TUESDAY, OCTOBER 12, 2010, AFTER SCHOOL. SO FAR
it has been a day of faith.

"Why is Mariah's bed gone?" Tyler asks when I walk in from work.

"Mariah's bed is gone?" I repeat.

"Yeah, her bedroom's empty."

Not that my son would lie, but I have to see this for myself. I run
upstairs to check.

All that's left in Mariah's room are candy wrappers, lost socks, and
dirt. Her bed has been sacrificed to The Game Gods.

"What's next?" Tyler asks. "Am I gonna come home after school
tomorrow and *my* bed will be gone too? Maybe I just won't come home
anymore." And I thought nothing ever rattled Tyler.

My first reaction is unbelief. Then horror. Then just plain anger. So
much for faith.

Mariah is at a friend's house, and Tyler is just leaving. I stomp down
to the laundry room where I know my husband is and demand, "Where's
Mariah's bed?"

"It's in the garage," he answers quietly.

"*Why?*"

"Shhh, Steven's still asleep. Let's go upstairs to talk." I sometimes
forget about Steven. He rarely comes out of his room.

I sit on the blanket-couch on the floor in the living room. He kneels
next to me and lays a hand on my shoulder, but I shrug it off. "So?" I ask.

He sits in the red chair and leans toward me. "We had four foster
children." He pronounces each word separately and deliberately.

"What does that have to do with Mariah's bed? They didn't sleep in it!"

"It's the number. We bought *four* beds and we had *four* foster children, and I've discovered four is a bad number. I tested it out to see if we were supposed to get rid of the beds. A black car left the cul-de-sac right after I put them in the garage. The wrong people will get points if we don't get rid of them."

"Bull crap!" I say. I stand up and point a finger at him. "You can't take Mariah's *bed* away from her! How do you think that will make her feel?"

Very calmly, he answers, "She's okay with it. She's not herself. She's acting as proxy for someone with ulterior motives."

That did it. I storm into the garage, my adrenaline pumping like a jackhammer. I pull out the base of Mariah's captain bed from the growing pile of casualties. It's bulky and heavy, but I don't care. I drag it, pull it, push it, heft it up to her room. I return for the bed boards, the headboard, the mattress. He doesn't even try to stop me.

But he's smiling. And nodding. "What?" I pant, out of breath.

"It's okay," he explains, still smiling. "As long as it's you and not me putting it back, it's okay to keep it."

Every particle of air I have in me I exhale in relief. It also occurs to me very quickly how this same concept can be of use in future negotiations with The Game Gods. I now have an ace up my sleeve.

Sure enough, while I'm at work on Wednesday, Tyler's mattress ends up in the garage, awaiting a verdict. I get home just in time to put the mattress back in his room before he walks in the door from school. I'm cool as a cucumber as he walks by and heads to his room.

***

It's nice to have a reprieve from the strangeness my world has become and write to Chandy. In my email, I give her a rundown of the family but leave out her father. I can't think of anything to say that isn't secret.

Wednesday, October 13, 2010

Dear Chandy,

Have you heard about the young lady Steven talks to that is from Victorville? Her name is Demi (I love it), and he says they talk (not text) for hours at a time on the phone. He seems pretty animated when he talks about her. He tried to call her one evening, but she was on another call, so at about 9:00, he was visiting with me and just waiting for the time he needed to leave for work. (He usually leaves around 9:30 since he works graveyard at Walmart.) Well, he suddenly stands up and says, "I'm leaving. I'm getting a phone call." And out the door he went. He still hangs out with George on Tuesdays and works Wednesday night through Sunday night.

I don't see much of Levi. He'll call occasionally. Like he called and said his car was struggling to start. I told him it sounded like a dead battery. Sure enough, it flat out died on him and wouldn't start at all. He put in a new battery and it's fine now. I wish he'd find some work, but I *am* glad that he's going to college.

Tyler has a diverse set of friends, and most of them live either in Ironwood or Santa Clara, so he's quite often gone. Last Friday night, he had five friends over. They ate nachos and chocolate chips (I didn't have any treats in the house) and then they went to the football game, I think. Tyler hates his French teacher, which is too bad. It would be fun to learn French if you had a good teacher. He is liking Theater Tech, though. He's helping with the set for *Peter Pan* in November.

Mariah's friends are as diverse as Tyler's. She has her friends here in the cul-de-sac, plus she still hangs out with Caroline occasionally. Then she has a bunch of friends in Santa Clara. If she's not hanging out with them, she's on FB with them. I don't ever see Mariah or Tyler doing homework, but they've always done well in school. Tyler had to redo a math test the other day, though. I'm glad he's willing to put in the extra effort to redo it and get a better grade.

Well, work is going well for me. Not much new going on. Church is about the same also. The kids have Friday and Monday off from school, so I'm sure they'll enjoy a nice long weekend. They've begged for a school holiday that we don't go anywhere, so that makes it easy for me! I guess they just want plenty of time to hang out with friends here in the area.

Well, I know there's not much exciting going on here. I'll make sure to let you know if there is anything newsworthy. :) Take care and be safe!

Love ya much,

Mom

After telling me all about what is happening in China, she writes in her email back, "How is Dad? Tell him happy birthday for me. It was good to hear about the kids."

***

It's Thursday afternoon, October 14, 2010, Curtis's forty-seventh birthday. My parents are in town and call to tell us they have a present for him.

They're coming over.

I grab a bucket and fill it with water and some cleaner and don rubber gloves and then start washing the bare walls.

I doubt I can explain the missing couch, though.

The doorbell rings. "Hi, Mom!" I give her a hug. My dad is outside talking to Curtis. Fortunately, Curtis has always spoken to my family, even when he had stopped talking to everyone else, including his own children.

Mom walks in the house. I smile to hide my nerves. She asks about the couch. I mumble something about how I've always hated it so we got rid of it. I hope she doesn't get a peek inside the garage where the couch skeleton lies battered and beaten from the blows of the ax. That would be a hard one to explain.

The kitchen table would also be hard to explain. Luckily, she doesn't ask about it.

I don't know if I can take this much longer. I'm having to pretend more and more that everything is okay when it's obvious that it's not.

I begin to plead with God to please let it end. My children are suffering because they don't understand why their dad won't talk to them. They can't understand his other strange actions, either. I can't explain anything to them because I am sworn to secrecy, and I don't take that lightly. I feel that to be loyal to my husband, I have to keep his confidence. So I tell *no one*. I talk to *no one* about The Game but my husband. I feel so alone.

16

"To follow by faith alone is to follow blindly." —*Benjamin Franklin*

IT'S FRIDAY.
I have no fight left in me.
Out goes my big chest of drawers.
We take another load to the thrift store.
The house is so empty.
It's Saturday.
He sits in the red chair.
The kids walk in and out like zombies.
There's no place to hide.
No place to run.
It's Sunday.
Church is awkward.
He speaks to no one.
I pretend.
The
phone
rings.

17

*"Reality is the leading cause of stress among those
in touch with it." —Lily Tomlin*

IT WAS SUNDAY, OCTOBER 17, 2010, WHEN MY MOM
called, only a month and a half after Curtis had lost his job at the
school district. So much had changed so quickly. She and Dad were
coming to St. George and wanted to know if they could meet me somewhere to talk. Alone. Without my husband or children.

They were coming that afternoon, so during church I had plenty of
time to think about their arrival and our upcoming chat.

I admit I was scared. What did they want to talk about? I had a
sneaking suspicion that it had to do with The Game, and I felt a bit squea-
mish as I thought of having to try to explain some of the strange things
going on at our house lately. But that couldn't be it—no one else knew
about The Game.

My mind ran through other possible scenarios. Was it something in
my conduct they wanted to correct? Did they want to talk to me about my
parenting skills? That made another batch of butterflies swish through my
stomach. But my parents had always stayed out of our business and let us
raise our family as we saw fit, so that didn't seem right either.

Then horror made my breath catch in my throat. Did one or the other
of them have a terminal illness? Did they want to discuss it with me first
before breaking it to my family? This brought actual tears to my eyes as I
thought of the likelihood of that possibility. My parents had been taking
short road trips together recently to nowhere in particular, just to get
away. I wondered if that was their way of crossing some things off of their
bucket list or spending some precious time together if one of them didn't
have much time left.

Not wanting to dwell longer on that thought than I had to, I went back to my first suspicion. My thoughts were never far from The Game, and Curtis's silence proved an unwelcome and constant reminder. He hadn't spoken to anyone when we entered the church building. If my parents began to ask me questions that were associated with The Game, how could I respond? I was sworn to secrecy. I felt sick just thinking about it as I bent over slightly and laid an arm across my stomach.

Four o'clock finally came. I don't know how I got out of the house alone, since Curtis usually wanted to stick close, but I managed to get out and drive to the park in town where my parents said they would meet me.

The beginning of our chat was extremely awkward.

"So, tell us how things are goin' at your place?" my dad said.

His question would have sounded innocent enough, if it were spoken in a normal setting during a normal conversation, but I had blankets instead of couches and a husband who wouldn't talk to his own children, so I knew the question had implied meanings that I wasn't ready to explore, so I lied.

"Things are fine. How are you guys doing?" I asked

"Oh, fine, fine," my dad returned.

My mom gave it a try next. "Is there anything you'd like to talk to us about?"

Talk about a loaded question. They knew something. I knew they did, but I just didn't know how *much* they knew, and I was still torn between betraying my husband's trust and trusting my parents with my secrets. I'd had to keep so much to myself for so long that I began to wish I could open up. Still, I held back.

"I don't think so," I replied to my mom's question. Then I turned her question back on her. "Is there something that you'd like to talk to me about?"

My dad took the reins, but he was still backing into it slowly. "We've noticed some things about Curtis that we're concerned about."

"What do you mean? What kinds of things?" I asked.

"Well, the fact that he isn't working right now is one thing."

Tell me about it. If it concerns you, then imagine how much it concerns me, I thought.

I began to wonder if they were here just to see about the welfare of my family. I relaxed a little, knowing my parents had always helped us when we needed it. When I broke my leg, my mom spent weeks with me in Idaho, taking care of us while my husband stayed on at his job in St. George. Plus, my parents had offered to let us live with them until I had recuperated.

"Yeah, I know," I said, watching my fingers as I traced the pattern on the picnic table we were sitting at. "He'll be looking for something else soon." Another lie, but I wasn't about to tell them there would be no job hunting until after spring break of the following year.

"Curtis was different when we were in Church Wells," my dad tried again.

We had celebrated my grandma's ninetieth birthday the previous month in Church Wells, close to Lake Powell.

"What do you mean, 'different'?" I asked.

"Well, he not only acted a little strange, but there was something in his eyes. He looked a little crazed," my dad tried to explain.

"We've just been wondering if you've noticed anything unusual about Curtis lately, anything different at all," my mom chimed in, attempting to diffuse my dad's comment.

So this *wasn't* just about the welfare of my family, after all. My first suspicion had been correct. They knew something strange was going on, but they were going to have to drag the information out of me. I'd kept it a secret for nine years, and I wasn't about to spill the beans now.

"Curtis has always been awkward in social situations, you know that," I explained. "He has to make a joke out of everything to try to feel comfortable in a social setting."

"No, this was different than usual," my dad replied, shaking his head. I could tell he knew I was trying to defend my husband, but he wanted to get his point across. He was being very gentle and patient, not accusatory at all, and to see the way my parents cared so much was beginning to make me crack. I was having difficulty breathing and wouldn't look them in the eye. I gripped the rubber-covered mesh of the picnic table, sinking each finger into a different hole.

"Your couch and your table are missing," my mom nearly whispered. "Your walls are bare. Do you want to tell us why that is?"

That's all it took. The dam burst and I suddenly couldn't tell them fast enough.

"It's all part of something Curtis thinks is happening in our lives. It's been going on for years now, but since he was fired from his job, things have gotten worse."

"What do you mean, 'worse'?" my dad asked.

"Well, before now, Curtis would just talk about what he thought was happening, but since it hasn't happened the way he thought it would, he's begun to do things to try to speed it along. "

"What kinds of things?" my mom asked.

It was still a struggle to breathe, so my sentences were choppy and my voice sounded panicked and desperate.

"We've been taking loads and loads of stuff to the thrift store. Curtis feels like we're supposed to. He's getting rid of things in the house that he feels are associated with people that aren't supportive of us as a couple. The house is so bare now it echoes."

"That doesn't make any sense," my dad exclaimed sorrowfully.

"It gets worse," I continued. "Curtis isn't speaking to any of our children because he thinks they are standing in as proxy for people that he's not supposed to talk to." This is when my voice went high and tears began to fall.

"Oh, Pauline," my dad said with pure sympathy. That did me in. With tears streaming down my cheeks, I told them everything. My heart hurt a little to think I was betraying my husband's trust, but I had reached the end of my rope, and my parents were throwing me a lifeline. Had they not, I don't know how things would have turned out. As I explained some of the things Curtis felt were happening around us, like our van being bugged and our houses being wired, my dad brought up something I hadn't known about.

"Curtis sent me a letter," my dad explained. "He said that when I went to get my dental work done a few years back, he thinks they planted tracking and listening devices in my molar teeth." I was shocked and astounded! I hadn't a clue my husband had sent a letter like that to my dad. "After seeing Curtis last month and observing him closely, then putting things together with him being fired and all, we figured there was something going on that we thought we'd better try to get to the bottom of."

"Tell her what you think could be the cause of how Curtis has been acting," my mom urged my dad.

My dad likes to talk with his hands like I do, so he gestured with his large hands as he told me about the days before he started drilling wells.

"Back when I did cabinetry, I had to glue down countertops and other things with an extremely toxic glue. The fumes were horrible, and I remember one day getting dizzy and starting to hallucinate, it was so bad."

"That was when he decided he couldn't stay in cabinetry anymore and he bought the well-drilling business from Bill Peck," my mom supplied.

I wasn't sure where this was going, but I'd never heard my dad tell this story before, so I listened closely.

"There are certain chemicals that are dangerous to work around, like the chemicals in the glue I was using, and I'm pretty sure in Curtis's line of work, he has to use some pretty harsh chemicals too."

"That's true," I said in wonder. "He says that when he worked at Dixie High, when they refinished the gym floor it was sometimes 105 degrees in the gym because they couldn't turn on the air-conditioning or it would dry out the varnish too quickly. They applied the varnish on their hands and knees, so at times his face was within inches of the smell of the varnish."

"That's exactly what I'm talking about," my dad exclaimed. "Curtis has been exposed to some really bad chemicals, and it can even affect you when you get it on your skin. There's been studies of people that work in those kinds of conditions, and they've ended up with brain damage." He proceeded to tell me about a guy he had read about who had worked at Hill Air Force Base fixing aircraft engines. A certain chemical they used in those days was extremely toxic, and the effects on this man were horrible. "I think Curtis needs to see a doctor, and I'll bet we'll find out something."

I thanked my parents for coming and said an emotional good-bye, then went home with my thoughts in a whirl. I thought of how sad it would be to find out that my husband had suffered ill effects from his profession. *Brain damage?* Still, I was curious to find out what a doctor would say. On Monday, I called and made an appointment for a week from Wednesday, not knowing beforehand if Curtis would agree to go or not.

Monday, October 18, 2010

Dear Ma,

[After telling me all about her experiences in China]

I hope good things are happening at home, not bad. I love you and the family!

Take care, Chandy

Oh, if she only knew.

***

My schedule at Valor Hall, a private charter school where I worked as a teacher's aide, was from 8:00 a.m. to 1:00 p.m., so once I had returned from work on Monday, I immediately called my sister, Stephanie. I had wanted so desperately to tell her everything I had been going through. I always told her everything that was going on in my life. Except this. Now, I finally felt like I could. After talking to my dad it seemed so obvious that Curtis's dreams were nothing more than that, and knowing for certain now that they were false, I felt freed from the obligation of secrecy.

Just in case anyone were to come home while I was talking on the phone, I went for a walk while I spoke to my sister. A very long walk. We ended up talking for over an hour while I cried and poured my heart out to her. It was such a relief to finally be able to share the burden of what I had been experiencing with someone, just as it was a relief to finally tell my parents.

I felt it was better, however, to *not* tell some people.

Tuesday, October 19, 2010

Dear Stephanie,

Here's the latest from Chandy (I had forwarded the last email I received from Chandy to her). I am not really excited about the situation she is in. I really don't think it is at all professional to send someone into a strange land without much to go on. And why would you? I guess it's like Chandy says, Wendy wants to "spread the light," but it just seems so unorganized. I'm glad Chandy is taking it as well as she is. At least, I hope she's not just covering up if things are actually a lot worse. Like I am, I guess. Now I know what they mean in novels when they don't tell someone (that's away from home) something that's going on back at home because it would just worry them needlessly. Would YOU think I should say anything to Chandy about what's going on? I don't even really know how it is all going to turn out, plus she has plenty she has to worry about herself.

So, for now, I am just going to let things ride. I do think I am going to talk to the kids, though. Maybe they can be a positive influence on Curtis, say like, "I love you, Dad," on the way out the door, even though they figure he most likely won't answer.

The week following my parents' visit was a nightmare. On Wednesday, I told all the kids to meet me at the Center Square Park in St. George.

I needed to tell them everything. Steven and Levi were already in town doing something or other, so I called them on their cell phones to let them know where to meet. Curtis wanted to go anywhere I went, except when I went to work, so I don't know how I managed to get out of the house without him. He probably knew we were sneaking out to go talk about him, since he wasn't invited along, but it had to be done.

When I met up with the kids at the park, they looked completely baffled. I had never requested a clandestine conference with them before, and they must have wondered what I needed to talk to them about. Not unlike when my parents had called and asked to meet with me alone to talk.

Their reactions were all different when I told them that their dad had something wrong with him. Levi was like, "Yeah, whatever." He acted annoyed that we even had to talk about his dad at all. I hoped eventually he and Curtis would have a better relationship than they did at that time. Tyler and Steven were both very sensitive and understanding. Mariah was pretty quiet. She was still so young; I doubt she could really comprehend what was going on.

I let the kids ask any questions they wanted, but so much was left unanswered because we didn't really know yet what was going on with Curtis, and I couldn't answer their questions about what our future held. That was something I had yet to figure out. And later on, after our little meeting, it was all I could think about.

We already knew we were losing our home through that short sale, so a move was inevitable, but where would we go? What would Curtis do for work, if anything? I had no idea what he would be capable of now. My future was so uncertain, and I had no idea how to make some of the necessary decisions.

I had no clue how much longer we would be allowed to stay in our home, but I missed having the decorations and pictures on the walls, so I put everything back in place. I shouldn't have bothered.

***

Somehow I made it through my work week at Valor Hall even though I was a frazzled mess. On Friday, which was my day off, I called Curtis's brother, Corey, at the elementary school where he worked and asked if I could stop by to chat with him. We stood out on the playground for over an hour while I told him about everything that had been going on lately and about the things our family had been through in the past years. I cried, like I always did, when I told Corey that Curtis wasn't speaking to any of his children.

By the weekend, my stress level had gone through the roof, but I tried to remain calm for the sake of the family. Saturday mornings were something I always looked forward to, though, since Curtis and I helped run a volunteer Bountiful Baskets site, where the community would come to the site and pick up fruit and vegetable baskets they had ordered. For some reason, Curtis had never kept up his discipline of not speaking to anyone on these mornings. He conversed freely with the volunteers, and for two short hours every two weeks, I had my husband back.

I spent all day Saturday doing research on a computer at the library. I began to look for jobs that my husband could apply for, full-time jobs I could apply for, homes for rent, even apartments for rent if it came down to it—whatever would be the cheapest. Although I hated to do it, I told the two older boys, Steven and Levi, that they would most likely need to find a place of their own to live so that we could look for something smaller and less expensive for the remaining four of us. Levi had just graduated from high school and was now attending college, and Steven worked at Walmart. They were old enough to be out on their own.

On my way home that day, I called my parents to ask for advice. All the research I had done had led to dead ends. Nothing seemed like it would work for us. My dad answered the phone, and, with feeling, he asked me how I was doing. His concern did me in again, and as the tears started up, I managed to choke out, "I can't eat. I can't sleep. There's a constant knot in my stomach that never goes away."

"I don't doubt you feel that way," he said sorrowfully. "So, do you know what you're gonna do?" he asked.

"I don't know," I responded sadly.

"Well, Mom and I have talked about it, and we want to let you know you're welcome to come and stay with us until you can get back on your feet again."

"Really?" I asked, warmed by their generosity.

"Think about it and let us know what you decide."

It didn't take me long to know that it was our best option to move in with my parents. I hated to impose on them again, like we did when I had a broken leg, but I didn't see any way around it.

Sunday was a blur. I'm sure we went to church that day, since there was little that kept me home from church, but I don't remember the specifics.

Sunday, October 24, 2010

Dear Chandy,

Well, darlin', I tried on the cell phone and on the house phone to call the number you listed, but it keeps saying, "Your call cannot be completed as dialed." I don't know what the problem is. I checked Google and it says that any international calls going out from the USA have to start with 011, but I tried that, and I tried it without that. Still, it didn't work.

We broke the news to the kids today. We're moving. Probably within one to three weeks, depending on how Dad's doctor appointment goes on Wednesday. If they say fresh country air and a slower pace will help cure Dad, then we'll be fine, but if they say that he needs something more for treatment, we might have more doctor appointments to go to. I'm still not sure of his diagnosis, but I do know that we will be moving to Cannonville, at least for a little while. After that, I'm not sure what, but I don't think we'll be moving back to the city. Mariah sobbed and sobbed when she found out. It made me cry to watch her cry. But I told her that after she gives Bryce Valley a chance, if she still hates it out there, we will see what else maybe can be done. If we don't stay there very long anyway, she would just stay with us and move wherever we move, but if we end up staying for a while, she says she wants to live with Stephanie. I'd rather have her at home, but we'll see how things go. Tyler is a trooper. I think he'll thrive anywhere. I know he'll miss his friends here, and I told him we can come back to visit. Same with Mariah. She has so many friends here, but I know she'll easily make friends anywhere. I know that doesn't mean she'll automatically like it. But she's just so likeable. Right now, we have to consider Dad.

There will be lots going on, lots of new experiences and different things than we are used to now, so I'll probably have quite a bit to tell you. I love you, Chandy! Take care!

Love,

Mom

Sunday, October 24, 2010

Hi Mom and Dad,

I thought I'd just give you some insight on a few things.

As Curtis and I were talking yesterday about the move and all that is involved, I wanted to know where he stood as far as his delusions were concerned. Okay, I admit it. I'm not going to tiptoe around it. And I decided that I had been doing that very thing with Curtis, so I got up the nerve and I just sat down with him yesterday morning, and I laid it all out. I brought up incident after incident and tried to explain that there was no hidden meaning, that it didn't all tie in, that everyone isn't after us. I was being calm but not avoiding anything. Well, he just nodded his head over and over. I didn't know if anything was getting through, but then he kept saying, "I just think we need to move to Cannonville. I just know it will be good for me. It's what I need right now." Well, later on in the day, it occurred to me that I need to test his willingness to discard his fantasies, because there were still some signs that he was holding on to them (like when we made the decision to move, I could tell he was watching the cul-de-sac for cars. A white one pulled in, white is okay, so he stayed with the plan). I've learned what the signs are, I just didn't know WHY they were going on. I still don't really know why, but at least I know there is something wrong.

Anyway, so I tested him with the theory about the kids, about talking to them. And a couple of other things. Well, at that time it was apparent that he hadn't let go of anything, and for all I knew, moving to Cannonville was just a safety net for him to give this "game" or "test" a chance to wrap itself up and come to fruition. I was furious! I said, "Forget it! We're not moving! It will just be enabling you to hang on to everything and not let go of it all!" Well, he got this panicked look on his face, a look that seemed to say I was taking away his only lifeline, and he'd drown without it. And when he started talking, I understood a little bit more about this scared look. I think he has an inkling that something is amiss with himself, but he just doesn't quite know what it is or what to do about it. He launched into a long and detailed horror story about the horrific childhood he had and what a miserable father he had. For the first time ever, he calls him the "sperm donor." He wasn't speaking bitterly, just very hurt and frustrated. He says he spent the first half of his life fearing his father and trying to do anything to gain his approval but never succeeding, and now he's spent the second half of his life hating himself for hating his father and thinking that he was an awful person because he can't find it within himself to find any good about his dad.

When he was telling me these horrific stories from his childhood (he's told me many of them, but even some of these were new), he started tensing up and shaking and he couldn't even breathe very well. He finally admitted that he just wants to get away from anyone that will even think to ask him how his parents are doing (so try not to bring it up) and away from people he will run into that he knows he has to put up a front around (he was always so popular in school, put in positions that he didn't even run for, pushed to the forefront, but he was frightened to death to be there). His anxieties are so real, and he can't shake them. He's spent far too long trying to put a good face on, be the funny guy, etc. And he's spent far too long holding in all the hurt, because, "It's not manly to admit you're hurting, physically or emotionally. It's not manly to be sick. It's not manly to be a wimp and not work as hard as you possibly can as fast as you possibly can." He knows now that he has got to change. He also said he knows that you get 80% of your personality by the time you are six years old and to truly change after that takes nothing less than a miracle. Or a huge wake-up call, or something life changing or very dramatic that happens in your life. So he knows this is a very big thing. A very hard challenge. But he knows he's got to make some changes and he says he feels the only way that will happen is if he gets away and decompresses. If you think about it, we could all probably agree that he could use decompressing. He's always been so amped and taut as a drum. He didn't know any better. And it was drilled into him from the time he was FOUR years old. He could do 110 perfect push-ups when he was four years old. That's not a good thing. "If some is good, more is better" until you give yourself two hernias, shin splints, a torn-up shoulder, flat feet, and possible brain damage (or whatever it is we are dealing with). There's a lot of psychological stuff going on here, traumatic events from his childhood. Well, he was never a child. He worked at the fruit stand at age ten, the gas station at age twelve, when he was told he had to buy everything he needed from then on, and on and on he worked and worked. I'm not telling you this for pity. Just for background and information.

When I got off the phone with the two of you yesterday, Curtis asked how you sounded, and I said you sounded really upbeat and positive, and he actually teared up for a split second and said that it made him feel so much better to hear that. And even on the bedroom thing. The last thing he wants to do is be a burden, and he only feels we should make this move because he is unsure what else to do. When I had mentioned that Curtis said we would just stay downstairs so we aren't a bother, he was happy to hear that Dad said we should take the upstairs bedroom. He's anxious to help around, but he knows that even in that, he is going to have to change. It used to be jump in and get it done. Work hard, don't think. Now he knows he needs to just slow down and think through things, and he actually wants Dad to point things out, and say something like, "Have you thought of doing it this way?" or "What about this?" and just show Curtis how to see things better and think through things better. He wasn't ever taught to slow down and think through anything.

Anyway, I'm rambling. I just don't really get a chance to say all this on the phone, and even if I tried, I probably wouldn't remember it very well. Curtis is so amazing, and I know you know that. He's worth whatever it takes to help him get through this. I'm with him through it all. There's no other place I would rather be. We know we are meant to be together. We'll get over this bump. Thank you so much for all you have done for us, for all you are now offering to do for us. You have been the most incredible parents; none could be better. I love you tons!

Love,

Pauline

P.S. By the way, you can reply with anything you need to over this email. I'm the only one that uses it.

All the while, Curtis was still sitting in his chair, contemplating whatever it was he was thinking about, but he *knew* he couldn't say *anything* to me about The Game anymore, so suddenly, we had nothing to talk about. He only spoke if I spoke to him. The Game was far from over, as far as Curtis was concerned. I could tell by how he avoided the subject now and how he still didn't have anything to say to any of the kids. It was hard for me to be worried sick about my husband but not be able to talk to him about it. I felt like I was harboring a deep, dark secret about him that I only spoke to everyone else about behind his back. We used to be in on the secrets together, but now I felt like I was against my husband, and it hurt. I knew this was the beginning of the end, though, and that was a huge relief.

I was supposed to go in to work again Monday, and, for the sake of being able to get out of the house without Curtis, I pretended that I was going to work, but all I did was go in to give my resignation and then began the tedious process of shutting off the electric and water, forwarding our mail, and everything else required with a move. This was when I wished I had just left everything boxed from when I had taken everything off the walls. Still, if I had to look at the bright side, there *was* a lot less stuff to pack, since we had already donated so much of it to The Game Gods.

Tuesday, October 26, 2010

Dear Pauline,

We read your letter and want you to know that we love you both very much, and we are happy that we have room here for you all to stay. The road may be rough, but when we work together, we can make it through. This will be new to all of us. "The best is yet to come" as we have heard.

Bless your heart! Be strong and of a good courage. We all need to simplify our lives and find out what things are most important.

Onward and upward!

Lots of Love,

Mom

***

On Wednesday, October 27, 2010, it was time for Curtis's doctor appointment. Wanting to be sure Curtis would indeed go to his appointment, my dad and Curtis's brother, Corey, had met with him to persuade him to go. When my dad and Corey left, the first thing Curtis said was, "I'm not crazy!" It was difficult to help him understand that we just wanted to know if the chemicals he'd been working with had affected him in any way. It took much pleading from me, but he finally agreed to go.

Before going to the doctor's office, Curtis told me, as he had many times, about all the aches and pains he had been living with for years now—his torn rotator cuff, his poorly healed hernia, his shin splints, and so on. He said that the only way he would go to the doctor was if he could get those areas addressed. I let him believe that those things would be looked at, but I still needed a way to let the doctor know Curtis's symptoms, so I typed up a three-page description of everything that seemed strange or different about Curtis compared to when we were first married. One big difference was how he used to talk to everyone he came in contact with, and now he talked to no one. Another was the fact that he had always been so determined to work hard for a living, but now he was content to be at home, all day every day, sitting in his red chair, contemplating the colors of vehicles in the cul-de-sac.

The more things I listed, the more clear they suddenly became. While I had found some of the things Curtis told me extremely difficult to believe over the years, I hadn't ever questioned his health or wellness. It never occurred to me, *ever*, that there may be something truly amiss with Curtis. Yes, there was the occasional odd occurrence, and his unwavering belief that money was coming our way was definitely a bit odd, but most days he had seemed so normal. Everything else I attributed to his extreme tendencies. Maybe not at the very end, but by then, I'd had my own dream and had switched into survival mode, not knowing what else to do. Now that I could finally see the big picture, things began to add up, and I had a sneaking suspicion about what might be going on, so I checked out some books on mental illness from the library. Curtis caught me reading one and again said, "I'm not crazy!"

"I know you're not," I calmly replied. "No one said you are."

He must have believed me because he didn't press the issue.

When we arrived at the doctor's office, I secretly gave the pages I had typed to the nurse.

SYMPTOMS

- Feels like we are people of great interest.
- Feels as though we will be greatly blessed monetarily.
- Thinks our home has a high-powered camera on it. They watch our every move.
- Thinks everyone is in on this big game, or test, that we have to see through to its end.
- We can't ignore it. It will never go away. It will always follow us.
- Has answered some unknown voice out loud. Once he said, "Okay" and once he said, "No" when he didn't know I was listening.
- Odd speech. He likes to be vague, won't say names, even when it's someone we know well.
- Doesn't have any close friends. More so lately. We used to be more in contact with his brother's family that lives in town, but not anymore. Same with some old high school friends. Doesn't talk to anyone at church.
- Does things ritualistically. He started wanting me on his right.

He passes other women on his left, even if he has to turn and walk backward for a bit. He swept to the left at the school because he said he was supposed to.

- He spends a lot of time in a recliner we have, hours and hours, usually just thinking, but now he is reading more. He never used to be able to sit hardly at all. He used to hold down two or three jobs. Now he's been without a job for over two months and he would have been way restless before.

- He sat in a closet last spring and said he asked yes and no questions. He said if he just sat there, nothing would happen, but as soon as he started asking questions, a machine would surge, on the right for yes and on the left for no. He said he was talking "code talk" and that there was someone that answers him. He spent hours and hours and hours asking it questions. One to two hours during his regular work shift, then three to five hours per day on weekends for about five months. (It's *very* unusual for Curtis to be dishonest on his work hours and not put in a full day's work for a full day's pay, but he explained this away by saying, "They (his supervisors) know where I am and they *want* me to be in there."

- He said that he feels I have had "intrusions" that distorted my reasoning administered three different times in my body. Twice affecting my hormones, once a tracking/listening device placed in my molar teeth. He also feels he had the same placed in his molars. I asked what made him think so. He said he "asked." I said, "What made you think to ask such a question as that?" He said, "I wanted to know what was wrong with me." Feels like about twelve years ago, he started feeling different—more anxious, worse temper. He wrote a long letter to my father about it that I didn't know about. This is how we finally decided that something wasn't quite right. My dad put two and two together.

- When I have tried to talk him out of these delusions, he won't believe me at all. He says things like, "There are some things I *know* for sure. I *promise.*"

Details of the "Game" or "Test" we are supposedly experiencing and have been for about eight years:

- Thought our children were given alternate personalities, that they were acting proxy for someone with ulterior motives: women that were "after" him, men that were after me, and that if we spoke to them, it would give the wrong people points. He hasn't spoken to his children for nearly two months. He also did not speak to his Sunday School class, at all, for three Sundays in a row. He thought they were also standing proxy for people with ulterior motives.

- Can only go shopping from 9:00 a.m. to 12:00 p.m. on Friday That's the only time that we have been given protection for while we are away from the house.

- Would not talk to anyone at the high school for the last few weeks last year and first few weeks this year because he didn't want to give the wrong people points. He couldn't decipher who was okay to talk to and who wasn't, so he just didn't talk to anyone.

- We have taken a load to the thrift store nearly every Friday for many weeks. Says that the more we get rid of the better, and to get rid of anything that might tie in to anyone who isn't "for us." Says they set aside our stuff at thrift store and it is auctioned off because anything that we once owned is of great interest.

- Cars that drive in and out of our cul-de-sac have meaning. The colors have meaning. Black and red are not good signs. White is okay. He makes decisions based on this coming and going.

- Said when I was out of the house, he spoke to someone, face to face, about this "test." Won't tell me who. He says he can't tell me. He is asked questions and has to "report back" so he has limitations of what he can tell me. When he goes for walks, he says he talks to someone. Sometimes very quick, sometimes a little longer. Won't tell me who. He'll tell me a new thought or an answer to a particular criterion he was wondering about, and I'll ask how he knows that. He says he asked the "orchestrators" of this test. But he hadn't gone anywhere.

- We only talk about this "game." Sometimes one to two hours per day. We rarely talk about anything else. Explaining the ins and outs and procedures, criteria we are supposed to follow, and what the rewards will be if we can be strict and not give the wrong people points.

- Often talks about what he wants to do with the money and feels he can help many people when times get harder.

- Numbers have been a big deal. Certain numbers have been

"bought up," you might say, by those with ulterior motives. Numbers 2, 4, 7, and 8 are not good numbers. When do errands, we must have three or five places to go. He counts every item in the shopping cart and if there are forty-four, he says to get one more thing. Prices of items couldn't have only the bad numbers. Quantity purchased of any item couldn't be a bad number. We could only go to certain check stand numbers, certain parking stalls, and movies at certain times. For a while, he even timed his bathroom visits *on* the bad numbers, as a sort of negative effect.

- Overly obsessed with single women being interested in him and single men interested in me. When he coached track, he just knew this was true because he coached an excessive amount of young girls that had single moms. He also thinks some people are in a pseudo-marriage, just so that they look like they are "marryable."

- When this game concludes, it will be in a stage setting. Someone who lives around here and is a celebrity will be the host. (He won't say whom.) We will be called to the stage, and we will be asked who the top three people we are interested in (beyond our spouse) are, so that there is some monetary gain for those people that he thinks deserve it and that have good intentions (in other words, they would only be interested in one of us if our spouse were to pass away or if we were to get a divorce.) These people in pseudo-marriages are in the running for the monetary gain because they are only in their marriage for show. There are highly influential people who are very wealthy that have invested in this game, and the more they invest, the more control they have, and the more strict criteria we are required to follow, to keep the game interesting and to keep people interested in continuing to invest. Last count, we would receive thirty-three million dollars. About five years ago, it was at four million.

POSSIBLE TRAUMA

- Head trauma—very hard bang to the forehead with the back end of a pickax, probably about twelve to fourteen years ago.
- Toxic chemical use—has worked for the school district for twenty-one years. Back in the nineties, they had very little money for product, so they did things the cheap way. They used paint thinner to strip the gym floor. He said he didn't wear the

protective mask because they couldn't have the air on while they were working because it dried out the paint thinner too fast to work with. So it was 95 to 105 degrees and they worked nine-hour days. Plus the product put back onto the gym floor was very strong. Many other products he used were very strong and toxic.

When we were called back to the exam room and the doctor joined us, Curtis immediately went into all of his ailments and complaints and asked if there was an operation that could help. After ten or fifteen minutes of this, he still hadn't lost any steam at all, so I finally spoke up and said, "Yes, hon, but why are we really here?" I had watched earlier in the hall as the doctor glanced through the pages I had typed, so I knew he knew what I meant.

Curtis didn't answer, so I spoke up and said the first thing that came to mind. "Curtis thinks we're going to receive thirty-three million dollars."

The doctor turned to Curtis and asked, "Why do you think that, Curtis?"

"Because of some dreams I've had."

"Tell me about your dreams," said the doctor.

Curtis proceeded to tell the doctor of the experiences we'd had in the past years. Whenever Curtis was vague, which was common for him, I would clarify, such as describing the structure of The Game, the orchestrators who had set it all up, that Curtis thought we were being tested, and the investments involved.

After about a twenty-minute visit, the doctor just blurted out, "Well, it looks to me like what we have here is a case of paranoid schizophrenia."

There it was: his diagnosis. Suddenly, everything I had experienced for the last nine years with Curtis, every strange, unfathomable dream he'd had and date he'd predicted, had an explanation. Something that made it all make sense, which was a good thing, yet the diagnosis wasn't good. What I'd read in the books on loan from the library was that schizophrenia is hereditary and gets worse over time.

As we left the doctor's office, I asked Curtis if he was ready to admit that The Game was a complete hoax because of the doctor's diagnosis.

"They got to him too," was Curtis's reply. Now that I knew more about the symptoms of paranoid schizophrenia from reading the library books, I knew what he meant. Curtis actually felt like someone had told the doctor to pronounce that diagnosis. In other words, he was flat-out in denial.

"I can't have schizophrenia," Curtis told me while we were driving home from the doctor. "They wear big coats and walk around mumbling to themselves."

It was true. We knew of a schizophrenic who was well known in St. George because he constantly walked the streets, and we knew he was schizophrenic through the grapevine. He'd always wear a big, heavy coat, even in July, and you could see him talking to himself, gesturing with his hands. He was unshaven and had long, bushy hair.

They don't teach Schizophrenia 101 in college, so before Curtis, the man in St. George was my only association with the disease. It was just a word, another illness that somebody else had.

Then there was the fact that I had been sworn to secrecy, so although there were times that I wanted to ask someone or call a nurse or my dad about some of the strange things Curtis was doing, my loyalty won out, and I went without information for all of those years. That my husband's new odd beliefs and behaviors stemmed from what he'd heard and seen in dreams was also problematic. In our religious culture, it is accepted that dreams could be the delivery system for spiritual manifestations from God, so to accept them as divine revelation was normal. It's as if everything was stacked against us.

For the most part, too, life was fairly normal, until those last few months. Then things got so bad, it almost seemed *too* strange to tell anyone about. I had told tiny bits and pieces to my sister throughout the years, but she had never guessed a mental illness was involved either. I remembered that Curtis's mother had been on medication for schizophrenia, but it didn't really stand out among all the other things she took meds for. It was just another word, another ailment, something akin to anxiety, I thought.

Now that I knew what it really meant and that my husband had it, I was bewildered and heartbroken. This was a lifetime deal—no cure.

I knew that my life would never be the same, and trying to imagine how things would turn out was impossible. But I also knew we didn't have to play The Game anymore—it didn't exist.

18

*"What surrounds us we endure better for giving it
a name—and moving on." —Emile M. Cioran*

WITHIN EIGHT DAYS FROM THE TIME CURTIS HAD
his doctor appointment, we were packed up and relocated.
Life seemed precarious at that point. Would Curtis ever be
able to hold down a job again? Would he need to be institutionalized or
put on medication?

I wanted all possibilities of brain damage from chemical use ruled
out, so I scheduled Curtis for an MRI. I was kind of hoping they *would*
find something, since that seemed preferable to a condition with symptoms that progressively worsened and may be inherited by our children.
The test came back normal.

The next step was counseling. We had three sessions with a wonderful
therapist, but Curtis didn't budge, not even a little bit. He knew what he
knew and no one could tell him otherwise. The only way to receive medication for his condition was to continue sessions with the therapist, who
could recommend a treatment to the doctor of psychology, who was the
only one that could make out the prescriptions. But Curtis was in denial
and absolutely refused to take any medication, so all we could do was go
home and hope his symptoms improved.

When we moved, Curtis began speaking to all of his children except
Mariah. He was still convinced that Mariah was a proxy for someone
who played on the opposing side in The Game—a twenty-three-year-old
Curtis had known when she was in high school. He still ran into her
on occasion and had passed her on the road one day. She waved at him
wildly from her car, which he must have construed as flirting. He was
concerned that she would attempt to break up our marriage, but it wasn't

until Curtis pulled into our cul-de-sac and saw one of the neighbor kids with the number 23 on his shirt that he knew this girl was against us. She had the first initial *M* and so did Mariah, so, naturally, Mariah must have been this girl by proxy.

Needless to say, when Mariah struggled with the move, Curtis wasn't there to help console her. I was on my own with this one, yet I was at a loss as to what I should do. Mariah sobbed every night for a week—huge, quaking sobs that wrenched my heart out. The thing was, Mariah never cried. She huffed when she was mad, was too tough to cry when she got hurt, and she was too young to have the kind of boy problems that girls cry over. We were breaking new ground here.

Mariah begged to go live with one of her friends back in Ivins or go live with Stephanie, but I couldn't bear to not have her at home with us. I told her she had to at least give it two weeks, and then we'd talk about it if she still wanted to go somewhere else. Luckily, some of the kids at her new school befriended her, and before long she was happy and loving it in our new town.

There was still the issue of Curtis not speaking to her, though. More than two months had gone by and this hadn't changed.

"Why aren't you speaking to Mariah?" I asked. I only got a shrug in return. This infuriated me! "It's not right, hon! Can't you understand how you're hurting her? And don't you dare tell me she's not hurting because she isn't herself!"

"It's not like I'm *not* talking to her," Curtis replied. "It's just that I don't have anything to say to her. We don't have anything in common. What would I say?"

"You're kidding, right? You're her *father*! Ask her how her day has been. Ask her how the night before went with her friends. Or you *could* tell her you love her. What a concept!"

"You don't have to raise your voice. I can hear just fine," Curtis complained.

"I can raise my voice if I want to!" I hollered. "You know darn well that you'd have at least *something* to say to Mariah if you weren't still trying not to talk to her!"

Another shrug.

I got a little mean. "If you're harboring thoughts that The Game is still going, then we need to get you on some medication so that you can start thinking straight!"

"That's not happening," Curtis said.

"This isn't fair. Not to me, not to Mariah!" I stood up and shook my finger at him. "You were diagnosed with paranoid schizophrenia! The *doctor* said you needed to get on some medication, and that if you did, you'd be able to live a fairly normal life. Don't you want that? I do!"

"I'm not going on medication, so don't bring it up again!" Curtis said firmly.

"Oh, for heaven's sake!" I flopped down on the couch in defeat. "Fine! No medication. But you have to at least start talking to Mariah, or I'll stop talking to you!"

I got up and stormed out the door to go pick up Bountiful Baskets in the neighboring town. When I returned, Curtis was standing in the doorway, smiling, with his arm around Mariah. I cried in relief.

Amazingly, Mariah never showed any bitterness toward her father for the way he had acted. It was as if nothing had happened; when Father's Day came, Mariah gave her dad a card with a personal note about how much she loved and appreciated him. I was in awe.

How fortunate I am to have such loving children. The other kids were very forgiving too and understood their dad couldn't help what he had done. Levi copped a bit of an attitude at first, but not for long. It didn't take much for Curtis and Levi's relationship to level out and get better. Steven had always been close to his dad, so that didn't change.

Poor Chandy, though. What a shock it was for her to come home and find out about her dad's diagnosis and realize that her family was moving! She had only been gone for five weeks, and so much had changed since she left. She came to our new home with us and stayed for about a week to visit. It was good for Mariah to have her big sister there for a while.

Luckily, Tyler and Mariah were quick to make friends and settle in. Everything fell into place for Curtis and me too. Within just a couple of weeks, I had secured a job at the local high school working as a paraprofessional in the special education department. Curtis was hired on by a local concrete company and did tree trimming on the side. We found a manufactured home for an incredibly low price and opted to move it onto my parents' large property so that we could live close.

Within two months from the time we moved in with my parents, we had a foundation poured, a septic tank installed, water and electricity routed to the site, and the home moved up to the property. It all came together unbelievably fast.

Although physically things were coming together well, mentally I found I was functioning on autopilot. The lifelong aspects of being married to someone with a mental illness came to me in degrees. My immediate worries were whether Curtis would ever be able to work a normal job again and whether The Game would ever really end for him. How would my neighbors react to his diagnosis? How would I help people understand Curtis's limitations in religious or civic functions?

Future worries were about how Curtis's illness would progress. What symptoms would he continue to have? What new symptoms might pop up? Was there any possible way he could get better?

In the meantime, we took life a day at a time. Curtis seemed to cycle for a couple of years. It seemed like once every week or so, he would act a little more off than usual. When in the presence of company, he continued to be a bit awkward, which he explained as his way of trying to feel comfortable in a new and unpredictable situation.

The trauma of everything I'd been through prior to Curtis's diagnosis, as well as his actual diagnosis and the ramifications that it brought, left me vulnerable in ways that occasionally blindsided me. One of the classes I attended as a paraprofessional was seventh-grade health, and part of the curriculum included a short movie about a schizophrenic, one of those ABC after-school specials they used to show on TV. The moment I heard that's what the teacher would be showing in class, I broke down in front of my supervisor. I told her there was no way I could handle watching something of that nature so soon after what I had gone through. Then I explained why. This was the first time I had mentioned anything about what our family had gone through. I hadn't told anyone, I think, except the secretary of the school, and I'd been working there for a couple of months. When people asked me what had brought us here, I would just say that we had always wanted to move to the country, which was true.

It took me nearly a year to get up the nerve to tell the rest of the people in the community the real reason we moved. It wasn't that I was ashamed, just that the wound needed time to heal, and I wasn't in a hurry to reopen it.

EPILOGUE

(Three years later)

WE LIVE IN A TINY TOWN NESTLED IN THE VALLEY of some of the most beautiful mountains on earth. At least we think so. If there is a perfect place to heal, this is it. When Curtis and I go for walks together now, it's not because we can't say certain things in the house. We go to enjoy the evening, where we are accompanied by chirping crickets and the breeze singing through the pine trees. It feels like heaven.

We live behind my parents in a perfect country setting—there's a workshop and a greenhouse, a chicken coop, an orchard, and a large garden spot. And a view to die for. Our front windows face a rock formation called Promise Rock, and the way the light plays on it and the surrounding mountains will take your breath away. We have two adopted stray cats named Squeaker and Bridget, and the times we look forward to the most are when we get the family together or talk to our kids on the phone. Curtis has rebuilt his relationship with all of his children, and they get along great. Having the kids come visit or hearing long phone conversations between them and their dad makes me happier than it seemed would ever be possible again.

There is a 90 percent difference in my husband's symptoms. He is so much better now. Where he used to cycle (have bad days) every week or so, that time frame was reduced to every two weeks about a year ago. Now it only seems to be about once a month. The little things that still come up are those things that I will have to adjust to for the remainder of our lives, things like how Curtis will not ask for any days off at work because he's positive that it will get him fired, and the fact that he wears the same shirt every single day, whether he works or not, even when we go out on dates: long-sleeved, dark blue, cotton, button-down shirts. It seems to be a comfort to him, though. It's part of his routine he can count on, so I don't mind.

Still to this day, it sort of freaks me out when Curtis leaves his drawers just barely open. He'll do other things that don't make sense, like switching the toaster plug to the top outlet. I like it plugged in the bottom of the two outlets so I can have easy access to the top one when I need to plug in the popcorn popper or Crock-Pot. We played switcheroo a few times, and then I finally called him on it.

"Why do you keep moving the toaster plug to the top outlet?" I asked him.

He got a sheepish look on his face, but he wouldn't answer. I just shrugged and smiled.

The quirks that make up 10 percent of Curtis's personality are just that, quirks. Curtis can talk to almost anyone. He's intelligent, witty, and a riot to talk to! He's so good to me and we have such an amazing life together. He will always be my favorite person in the world. I love him like crazy, and as long as he is happy, I am happy.

While in my youth, when I had dreamed of what married life would be like, I always imagined it would be similar to what my parents had. In many ways it is; Curtis and I have a deep love for one another, we respect each other, and we work as a team to deal with what life sends our way. I've found, though, that I'm much different than my mother. Submissiveness has given way to assertiveness by way of necessity. Furthermore, I'm stubborn and like to have control. I didn't used to be like that. I was pretty naive and meek when I was first married. Through the years, though, Curtis has deferred to me on so many things that he was just too impatient to worry about. Bills large and small, everything to do with the finances, what home to buy, what car to purchase, where we should live, what to do during date night—it was all left up to me. I'm used to it now, but have to catch myself so that I'm not too much of a control freak.

Our day-to-day activity has been quite simplified. Curtis loves routine, needs routine. His stress level has to be almost zero, which means my stress level has to be almost zero. Often, he'll ask me how I'm doing. I'll say I'm fine and ask him the same, and then he tells me, "Now that I know you're fine, I'm fine."

Curtis has his own eating schedule and diet, including his workout routine and taking certain vitamins and herbs at certain times of the day, so it's rare that we all eat together as a family except on Sundays. While I'm pecking away at the keyboard or remodeling or reading a book or harvesting produce, he still spends a lot of time in the recliner—now brown since the red one broke—watching the news, surfing online for herbs and vitamins to purchase, reading, and studying his herb book. And dozing.

Curtis can still be stubborn, but I'm learning when I need to stand up to him and be aggressive. It's a difficult balance sometimes, knowing that Curtis is the head of the family and letting him have that role but also knowing a lot of the decisions will be deferred to me. One thing he will not do is discipline the kids. We have Tyler and Mariah still at home, and Steven, our oldest son, has moved in with us, but Curtis won't even ask them to help around the house. I didn't know specifically that he *wouldn't* discipline them, only that he *didn't*, until one day he told me the story. I mentioned to him that I had written about when he and Levi had the yelling match that ended with Levi punching a hole in the wall.

"After that day, I told myself something like that would never happen again," he said. "That's why I refuse to discipline the kids. I'm not going to take that chance."

Therefore, I set curfews, dole out consequences for broken curfews, assign chores, and say yea or nay to each and every request my kids make. I've tried a couple of times to hand off the responsibility to Curtis when they've asked me for something that I really didn't want to decide alone, but he always says yes, so what's the point? It's tough having to be the bad guy every time, but someone's gotta do it, and in some ways, having the control can be nice too.

When I read or hear schizophrenic horror stories in books that I've ordered or in online forums, I realize that I am actually very fortunate. There are so many unfortunate circumstances out there—repeated hospitalizations, trial and error with medication—and quite often divorce ensues when one person in a marriage is schizophrenic. I can't help but be grateful for my own circumstance. Curtis treats me like gold. He's extremely affectionate and expressive when it comes to telling me how glad he is that he married me and how much I mean to him.

I've never once wished my life had turned out differently. We've been through a lot, but who hasn't? I thank the good Lord for sending me

Curtis and my five beautiful children. I couldn't have asked for a husband that worked harder to provide for our family. Plus, I'm happy to say we have laughter back in our lives. Curtis sure knows how to make me laugh. Oh, can he make me laugh! The sore-gut-streaming-tears kind of laugh! And I love it.

ABOUT THE AUTHOR

PAULINE HANSEN GREW UP IN A TINY TOWN WHERE she went everywhere barefoot, played in the ditch, and anticipated the arrival of the bookmobile every two weeks. Her love of reading led her to dream of someday becoming an author. In addition to reading and writing, Pauline enjoys traveling, spring cleaning, cooking, organizing, and spending time with her family. After nearly twenty-five years of living in the city, she now resides once again in her tiny hometown in southern Utah with her husband, three of their five children, and two cats. *Patchwork Reality* is her first publication.

0 26575 13644 9